Of Other Worlds

ESSAYS AND STORIES

Of Other Worlds

ESSAYS AND STORIES

C. S. Lewis

edited by
WALTER HOOPER

What if within the Moones faire shining spheare?
What if in every other starre unseene
Of other worldes [we] happily shoulde heare?

SPENSER
(*The Faerie Queene* II Prol. 3)

A Harvest Book
HARCOURT BRACE JOVANOVICH
New York and London

Printed in the United States of America

Library of Congress Cataloging in Publication Data
Lewis, Clive Staples, 1898-1963.
    Of other worlds.
    (A Harvest book ; HB 317)
    Includes bibliographical references.
    I. Title.
[PR6023.E92603 1975]   823'.9'12   75-6785
ISBN 0-15-667897-7

First Harvest edition 1975

A B C D E F G H I J

PREFACE

'You can't get a cup of tea large enough or a book long enough to suit me,' said C. S. Lewis. And he meant it, for at that moment I was pouring his tea into a very large Cornish-ware cup and he was reading *Bleak House*.

This little anecdote suggests, I think, a theme for this book: the excellence of Story. And especially those kinds of story we call fairy tales and science fiction, both of which were dear to Lewis. In the nine essays printed here he discusses certain literary qualities which he feels critics neglect. Also—something rare with Lewis—he talks a little about his 'Chronicles of Narnia'[1] and his science fiction trilogy. Indeed, I have felt it so important to preserve in a permanent form all that Lewis has written about his own fiction that I have considered their publication, despite the overlapping in several of the pieces, justified. Following the essays are three science fiction short stories (as far as I know, the only short stories of Lewis's ever to be published) as well as the first five chapters of a novel which Lewis was writing at the time of his death.

Lewis's boyhood stories, written (I think) between the ages of about six and fifteen, were about his invented Animal-Land and the anthropomorphic beasts which inhabit it. His brother had, as his own country, India. In order that it might be a shared world, India was lifted out of its place in the real world and made into an island. Then, the mood of the systematizer being strong in both boys, Animal-Land was united with India to form the single state of Boxen. Soon the maps of Boxen included the principal train and steamship routes. The capital city of Murray had its own newspaper, *The Murray Evening Telegraph*. And so, out of an attic full of commonplace children's toys came a world

---

[1] Seven fairy tales which, according to Lewis, should be read in the following order: *The Magician's Nephew* (1955), *The Lion, the Witch and the Wardrobe* (1950), *The Horse and His Boy* (1954), *Prince Caspian* (1951), *The Voyage of the 'Dawn Treader'* (1952), *The Silver Chair* (1953), *The Last Battle* (1956).

as consistent and self-sufficient as that of the *Iliad* and the Barsetshire novels.

There are a good many stories and histories of Boxen extant (but unpublished) written in ruled exercise books in a large, neat handwriting and illustrated with his own drawings and water-colours. As the early legends of King Arthur and his Court grew to include romances of individual knights of the Round Table, so a systematic reading of Boxoniana from beginning to end (which, believe it or not, covers over seven hundred years) reveals a similar kind of growth. Lewis's interest was at first primarily that of tracing the history of Boxen; but once it became a finished creation, he turned to writing novels in which the principal characters—some little more than names in the histories—spring into prominence.

Lewis's masterpiece, and obviously the character he liked best, is Lord John Big. This noble frog is already the Little-Master, i.e. the Prime Minister, when we meet him in *Boxen: or Scenes from Boxonian City Life* (in two volumes complete with List of Contents, List of Illustrations, and Frontispiece). Later he has his own history: *The Life of Lord John Big of Bigham by C. S. Lewis in 3 Volumes* published by the 'Leeborough Press'. It is obvious, no doubt, from the titles that Lewis liked even the *making* of books. Drawn on the fly-leaf of one little book is the head of a spectacled mouse between the words 'Trade Mark'.

There is much to admire about Boxen. Lord Big is indeed a frog of powerful personality, and I find him almost as unforgettable as Reepicheep the Mouse and Puddleglum the Marshwiggle of the Narnia stories (who were, by the way, Lewis's favourites). There is not the slightest bit of evidence on a single page of the juvenilia that the author had to labour to find 'filling' for his really good plots: the stories seem to write themselves. And the humour, which is inseparable from the story itself, is unmistakably of the Lewis kind.

But, as Lewis himself admits,[1] Boxen is empty of poetry and romance. It would, I believe, astonish the readers of the Narnia books to know how really prosaic it is. This is (I think) chiefly because of his desire to be very 'grown-up'. He says himself, 'When I began writing stories in exercise books I tried to put

[1] *Surprised by Joy: The Shape of my Early Life* (1955), p. 22.

off all the things I really wanted to write about till at least the second page—I thought it wouldn't be like a grown-up book if it became interesting at once.'[1] Most of all, the Boxoniana are blighted by, of all things, politics—something which Lewis came to detest later in his life. It did, after all, hold him so long in bondage. The characters in *Scenes from Boxonian City Life* all relish a place in the 'Clique' though none of them, not even the author, appears to have any clear idea what a 'clique' is. Which is not surprising for, as Lewis wanted his characters to be 'grown-up', he naturally interested them in 'grown-up' affairs. And politics, his brother says, was a topic he almost always heard his elders discussing. There are, by the by, *no* children in any of these stories.

A sentence in a piece of juvenilia which points to the future chronicler of Narnia and lover of 'faery land' is to be found in *The Life of Lord John Big of Bigham* where Lewis puts into the mouth of the Little-Master these words: 'Say what he will, in every man's heart of hearts there is a deep-rooted objection to change—a love of old customs because of their age which neither time nor eternity can efface.'

One other comparison remains. Lewis, as a boy, seems to have had little feeling for the real nature of beasts as such. In the Boxen stories they are little more than 'dressed animals', and without the advantage of the illustrations one might find it difficult to remember that Lord Big is a frog, James Bar a bear, Macgoullah a horse, and so on. But it is as 'servants, playfellows, jesters' that we meet them in Narnia where there are 'wagging tails, and barking, and loose slobbery mouths and noses of dogs thrust into your hand' (*The Silver Chair*, p. 115). When Prince Caspian visits the tree-house of the Three Bulgy Bears, he is answered from within by a 'woolly sort of voice'; and when the bears come out 'blinking their eyes' they greet the Prince with 'very wet, snuffly kisses' and offer him some honey (*Prince Caspian*, p. 67). And Bree, who is as fond as any horse of sugar-lumps, rises up from his roll in the grass, 'blowing hard and covered with bits of braken' (*The Horse and His Boy*, p. 187).

There are, however, a few places in the juvenilia in which we

[1] 'Peace Proposals for Brother Every and Mr Bethell', *Theology*, vol. XLI (Dec. 1940), p. 344.

find that winsome commingling of beast and man—what Lewis might call 'Eden's courtesy'—and which is so characteristic of his fairy tales. Viscount Puddiphat, a music-hall artist, is being wakened by his valet (the italics are mine):

> On a certain spring morning, the viscount's valet had entered his master['s] bedchamber with a cup of chocolate, and the ironed morning paper. No sooner had his step resounded on the floor than *a mass of feathers stirred in the large bed, and the owl raised himself on his elbow, with blinking eyes.*

The faerie element is absent from Animal-Land but this, in itself, does not prove that Lewis had to conceal his interest in fairy stories. After all, there are differences of *kind* and it would do harm to force them into competition. Lewis wrote another romance (unpublished) about Dr Ransom which falls, chronologically, between *Out of the Silent Planet* and *Perelandra*. Contrary to what might be expected, it does not have a theological theme. However, one truth that strikes me from comparing Boxen and Narnia is this: Boxen was invented by a boy who wanted to be 'grown-up'; the 'noble and joyous' tales of Narnia were created by one liberated from this desire. One wonders what different fruits Lewis's literary gifts would have borne had he not overcome the modern bugbear that fantastic literature is—in a contemptuous sense—'childish'. We can of course never know this: the important thing is that he did overcome it.

In introducing these essays and stories I should, at the same time, like to thank all those who have allowed me to reprint some of the papers in this book. (1) 'On Stories' was first published in *Essays Presented to Charles Williams* (1947) by the Oxford University Press. It was originally read, in a slightly fuller form, to a Merton College undergraduate literary society as 'The Kappa Element in Fiction'. 'Kappa' stood for κρύπτον—the 'hidden element'. (2) 'On Three Ways of Writing for Children' was read to the Library Association and published in their *Proceedings, Papers and Summaries of Discussions at the Bournemouth Conference 29th April to 2nd May 1952*. (3) 'Sometimes Fairy Stories May Say Best What's to be Said' first appeared in *The New York Times Book Review, Children's Book Section* (18

November 1956). (4) 'On Juvenile Tastes' is reprinted from the *Church Times, Children's Book Supplement* (28 November 1958) and (5) 'It All Began with a Picture . . .' is reprinted here from the *Radio Times, Junior Radio Times*, vol. CXLVIII (15 July 1960).

(6) 'On Critics' appears in print for the first time, as does (7) 'On Science Fiction', a talk given to the Cambridge University English Club on 24 November 1955. (8) 'A Reply to Professor Haldane', also published for the first time, is a rejoinder to Professor J. B. S. Haldane's article 'Auld Hornie, F.R.S.', *Modern Quarterly*, N.S., vol. I, No. 4 (Autumn 1946) in which he criticizes Lewis's science fiction trilogy: *Out of the Silent Planet, Perelandra*, and *That Hideous Strength*. I have not, however, thought it necessary to reprint Professor Haldane's article for Lewis makes the argument quite clear. Besides, the chief value of Lewis's reply is not in its polemical nature, but in the valuable light he throws on his own books. (9) 'Unreal Estates' is an informal conversation about science fiction between Lewis, Kingsley Amis, and Brian Aldiss. It was recorded on tape by Brian Aldiss in Lewis's rooms in Magdalene College, on 4 December 1962. It was first published under the title 'The Establishment must die and rot . . .' in *SF Horizons*, No. 1 (Spring 1964) and later as 'Unreal Estates' in *Encounter*, vol. XXIV (March 1965).

(10) 'The Shoddy Lands', a short story, first appeared in *The Magazine of Fantasy and Science Fiction*, vol. X (February 1956). (11) Lewis's next story, 'Ministering Angels', was set off by Dr Robert S. Richardson's article 'The Day after We Land on Mars' which was published in *The Saturday Review* (28 May 1955). Dr Richardson's article contains the prediction that 'If space travel and colonization of the planets eventually become possible on a fairly large scale, it seems probable that we may be forced into first tolerating and finally openly accepting an attitude toward sex that is taboo in our present social framework. . . . To put it bluntly, may it not be necessary for the success of the project to send some nice girls to Mars at regular intervals to relieve tensions and promote morale?'[1] Lewis

[1] Robert S. Richardson. 'The Day after We Land on Mars', *The Saturday Review*, vol. XXXVIII (28 May 1955), p. 28.

takes it from there in 'Ministering Angels' which was originally published in *The Magazine of Fantasy and Science Fiction*, vol. XIII (January 1958). (12) 'Forms of Things Unknown' is published for the first time.

(13) *After Ten Years* is an unfinished novel which Lewis began in 1959. Though he never abandoned the idea of finishing it, he could not think of how to continue the story. Lewis became very ill in 1960 and lived in comparative discomfort until his death in 1963. This may partially account for his inability to 'see pictures'—which was his usual way of writing stories. He usually wrote several drafts of a scholarly work such as *The Discarded Image*, although one draft was often sufficient for a work of fiction. And, as far as I know, he wrote only the single draft of *After Ten Years* which is published here for the first time. Lewis did not divide the fragment into parts (or give it a title); but, as each 'chapter' appears to have been written at a different time, I have decided to retain these rather natural divisions. The reader should be warned that Chapter V does not really follow Chapter IV. Lewis was anticipating the end of the novel, and had he completed it, there would have been many chapters between numbers IV and V.

Lewis discussed this work with Mr Roger Lancelyn Green, the author and formerly a pupil of Lewis's, and Dr Alastair Fowler, Fellow of Brasenose College, and I have asked them to write about the conversation they had with him. The nature of the story makes it important, however, that the reader should save Mr Green's and Dr Fowler's notes until last.

I have to thank Dr and Mrs Austin Farrer, Mr Owen Barfield, and Professor John Lawlor for the help they have given me in preparing this volume. I am also grateful to Mr Roger Lancelyn Green and Dr Alastair Fowler for their notes on *After Ten Years*. A large share of thanks also goes to my friend, Mr Daryl R. Williams, for his careful proof-reading. And it is to Major W. H. Lewis that I owe the pleasure of editing his brother's essays and stories.

Wadham College, Oxford.　　　　　　WALTER HOOPER
October, 1965.

CONTENTS

Part I
ESSAYS

ON STORIES

It is astonishing how little attention critics have paid to Story considered in itself. Granted the story, the style in which it should be told, the order in which it should be disposed, and (above all) the delineation of the characters, have been abundantly discussed. But the Story itself, the series of imagined events, is nearly always passed over in silence, or else treated exclusively as affording opportunities for the delineation of character. There are indeed three notable exceptions. Aristotle in the *Poetics* constructed a theory of Greek tragedy which puts Story in the centre and relegates character to a strictly subordinate place. In the Middle Ages and the early Renaissance, Boccaccio and others developed an allegorical theory of Story to explain the ancient myths. And in our own time Jung and his followers have produced their doctrine of Archetypes. Apart from these three attempts the subject has been left almost untouched, and this has had a curious result. Those forms of literature in which Story exists merely as a means to something else—for example, the novel of manners where the story is there for the sake of the characters, or the criticism of social conditions—have had full justice done to them; but those forms in which everything else is there for the sake of the story have been given little serious attention. Not only have they been despised, as if they were fit only for children, but even the kind of pleasure they give has, in my opinion, been misunderstood. It is the second injustice which I am most anxious to remedy. Perhaps the pleasure of Story comes as low in the scale as modern criticism puts it. I do not think so myself, but on that point we may agree to differ. Let us, however, try to see clearly what kind of pleasure it is: or rather,

3

what different kinds of pleasure it may be. For I suspect that a very hasty assumption has been made on this subject. I think that books which are read merely 'for the story' may be enjoyed in two very different ways. It is partly a division of books (some stories can be read only in the one spirit and some only in the other) and partly a division of readers (the same story can be read in different ways).

What finally convinced me of this distinction was a conversation which I had a few years ago with an intelligent American pupil. We were talking about the books which had delighted our boyhood. His favourite had been Fenimore Cooper whom (as it happens) I have never read. My friend described one particular scene in which the hero was half-sleeping by his bivouac fire in the woods while a Redskin with a tomahawk was silently creeping on him from behind. He remembered the breathless excitement with which he had read the passage, the agonized suspense with which he wondered whether the hero would wake up in time or not. But I, remembering the great moments in my own early reading, felt quite sure that my friend was misrepresenting his experience, and indeed leaving out the real point. Surely, surely, I thought, the sheer excitement, the suspense, was not what had kept him going back and back to Fenimore Cooper. If that were what he wanted any other 'boy's blood' would have done as well. I tried to put my thought into words. I asked him whether he were sure that he was not over-emphasizing and falsely isolating the importance of the danger simply as danger. For though I had never read Fenimore Cooper I had enjoyed other books about 'Red Indians'. And I knew that what I wanted from them was not simply 'excitement'. Dangers, of course, there must be: how else can you keep a story going? But they must (in the mood which led one to such a book) be Redskin dangers. The 'Redskinnery' was what really mattered. In such a scene as my friend had described, take away the feathers, the high cheek-bones, the whiskered trousers, substitute a pistol for a tomahawk, and what would be left? For I wanted not the momentary suspense but that whole

4

world to which it belonged—the snow and the snow-shoes, beavers and canoes, war-paths and wigwams, and Hiawatha names. Thus I; and then came the shock. My pupil is a very clear-headed man and he saw at once what I meant and also saw how totally his imaginative life as a boy had differed from mine. He replied that he was perfectly certain that 'all that' had made no part of his pleasure. He had never cared one brass farthing for it. Indeed—and this really made me feel as if I were talking to a visitor from another planet—in so far as he had been dimly aware of 'all that', he had resented it as a distraction from the main issue. He would, if anything, have preferred to the Redskin some more ordinary danger such as a crook with a revolver.

To those whose literary experiences are at all like my own the distinction which I am trying to make between two kinds of pleasure will probably be clear enough from this one example. But to make it doubly clear I will add another. I was once taken to see a film version of *King Solomon's Mines*. Of its many sins —not least the introduction of a totally irrelevant young woman in shorts who accompanied the three adventurers wherever they went—only one here concerns us. At the end of Haggard's book, as everyone remembers, the heroes are awaiting death entombed in a rock chamber and surrounded by the mummified kings of that land. The maker of the film version, however, apparently thought this tame. He substituted a subterranean volcanic eruption, and then went one better by adding an earthquake. Perhaps we should not blame him. Perhaps the scene in the original was not 'cinematic' and the man was right, by the canons of his own art, in altering it. But it would have been better not to have chosen in the first place a story which could be adapted to the screen only by being ruined. Ruined, at least, for me. No doubt if sheer excitement is all you want from a story, and if increase of dangers increases excitement, then a rapidly changing series of two risks (that of being burned alive and that of being crushed to bits) would be better than the single prolonged danger of starving to death in a cave. But that is just the point. There must be a pleasure in such stories distinct from mere excitement or I should not feel that I had been cheated in being given the earthquake instead of Haggard's actual scene. What I lose is the whole sense of the deathly (quite a different thing from simple danger of death)—the cold, the silence, and the surrounding faces of the ancient, the crowned and sceptred, dead. You may, if you please, say that Rider Haggard's effect is quite as 'crude' or 'vulgar' or 'sensational' as that which the film substituted for it. I am not at present discussing that. The point is that it is extremely different. The one lays a hushing spell on the imagination; the other excites a rapid flutter of the nerves. In reading that chapter of the book curiosity or suspense about the escape of the heroes from their death-trap makes a very minor part of one's experience. The trap I remember for ever: how they got out I have long since forgotten.

It seems to me that in talking of books which are 'mere stories'—books, that is, which concern themselves principally with the imagined event and not with character or society—nearly everyone makes the assumption that 'excitement' is the only pleasure they ever give or are intended to give. *Excitement*, in this sense, may be defined as the alternate tension and appeasement of imagined anxiety. This is what I think untrue. In some such books, and for some readers, another factor comes in.

To put it at the very lowest, I know that something else comes in for at least one reader—myself. I must here be autobiographical for the sake of being evidential. Here is a man who has spent more hours than he cares to remember in reading romances, and received from them more pleasure perhaps than he should. I know the geography of Tormance better than that of Tellus. I have been more curious about travels from Uplands to Utterbol and from Morna Moruna to Koshtra Belorn than about those recorded in Hakluyt. Though I saw the trenches before Arras I could not now lecture on them so tactically as on the Greek wall, and Scamander and the Scaean Gate. As a social historian I am sounder on Toad Hall and the Wild Wood or the cave-dwelling Selenites or Hrothgar's court or Vortigern's than on London, Oxford, and Belfast. If to love Story is to love excitement then I ought to be the greatest lover of excitement alive. But the fact is that what is said to be the most 'exciting' novel in the world, *The Three Musketeers*, makes no appeal to me at all. The total lack of atmosphere repels me. There is no country in the book—save as a storehouse of inns and ambushes. There is no weather. When they cross to London there is no feeling that London differs from Paris. There is not a moment's rest from the 'adventures': one's nose is kept ruthlessly to the grindstone. It all means nothing to me. If that is what is meant by Romance, then Romance is my aversion and I greatly prefer George Eliot or Trollope. In saying this I am not attempting to criticize *The Three Musketeers*. I believe on the testimony of others that it is a capital story. I am sure that my own inability to like it is in me a defect and a misfortune. But that misfortune is evidence. If a man sensitive and perhaps over-sensitive to Romance likes least that Romance which is, by common consent, the most 'exciting' of all, then it follows that 'excitement' is not the only kind of pleasure to be got out of Romance. If a man loves wine and yet hates one of the strongest wines, then surely the sole source of pleasure in wine cannot be the alcohol?

If I am alone in this experience then, to be sure, the present essay is of merely autobiographical interest. But I am pretty sure that I am not absolutely alone. I write on the chance that some others may feel the same and in the hope that I may help them to clarify their own sensations.

In the example of *King Solomon's Mines* the producer of the film substituted at the climax one kind of danger for another and thereby, for me, ruined the story. But where excitement is the only thing that matters kinds of danger must be irrelevant. Only degrees of danger will matter. The greater the danger and the narrower the hero's escape from it, the more exciting the story will be. But when we are concerned with the 'something else' this is not so. Different kinds of danger strike different chords from the imagination. Even in real life different kinds of danger produce different kinds of fear. There may come a point at which fear is so great that such distinctions vanish, but that is another matter. There is a fear which is twin sister to awe, such as a man in war-time feels when he first comes within sound of the guns; there is a fear which is twin sister to disgust, such as a man feels on finding a snake or scorpion in his bedroom. There are taut, quivering fears (for one split second hardly distinguishable from a kind of pleasurable thrill) that a man may feel on a dangerous horse or a dangerous sea; and again, dead, squashed, flattened, numbing fears, as when we think we have cancer or cholera. There are also fears which are not of *danger* at all: like the fear of some large and hideous, though innocuous, insect or the fear of a ghost. All this, even in real life. But in imagination, where the fear does not rise to abject terror and is not discharged in action, the qualitative difference is much stronger.

I can never remember a time when it was not, however vaguely, present to my consciousness. *Jack the Giant-Killer* is not, in essence, simply the story of a clever hero surmounting danger. It is in essence the story of such a hero surmounting *danger from giants*. It is quite easy to contrive a story in which, though the enemies are of normal size, the odds against Jack are equally great. But it will be quite a different story. The whole quality of the imaginative response is determined by the fact that the enemies are giants. That heaviness, that monstrosity, that uncouthness, hangs over the whole thing. Turn it into music and you will feel the difference at once. If your villain is a giant your orchestra will proclaim his entrance in one way: if he is any other kind of villain, in another. I have seen landscapes (notably in the Mourne Mountains) which, under a particular light, made me feel that at any moment a giant might raise his head over the next ridge. Nature has that in her which compels us to invent giants: and only giants will do. (Notice that Gawain was in the north-west corner of England when

'etins aneleden him', giants came *blowing* after him on the high
fells. Can it be an accident that Wordsworth was in the same
places when he heard 'low breathings coming after him'?)
The dangerousness of the giants is, though important, secon-
dary. In some folk-tales we meet giants who are not dangerous.
But they still affect us in much the same way. A *good* giant is
legitimate: but he would be twenty tons of living, earth-shaking
oxymoron. The intolerable pressure, the sense of something
older, wilder, and more earthy than humanity, would still
cleave to him.

But let us descend to a lower instance. Are pirates, any more
than giants, merely a machine for threatening the hero? That
sail which is rapidly overhauling us may be an ordinary enemy:
a Don or a Frenchman. The ordinary enemy may easily be
made just as lethal as the pirate. At the moment when she runs
up the Jolly Roger, what exactly does this do to the imagination? It means, I grant you, that if we are beaten there will be
no quarter. But that could be contrived without piracy. It is
not the mere increase of danger that does the trick. It is the
whole image of the utterly lawless enemy, the men who have
cut adrift from all human society and become, as it were, a
species of their own—men strangely clad, dark men with ear-
rings, men with a history which they know and we don't, lords
of unspecified treasure in undiscovered islands. They are, in
fact, to the young reader almost as mythological as the giants.
It does not cross his mind that a man—a mere man like the rest
of us—might be a pirate at one time of his life and not at another, or that there is any smudgy frontier between piracy and
privateering. A pirate is a pirate, just as a giant is a giant.

Consider, again, the enormous difference between being shut
out and being shut in: if you like, between agoraphobia and
claustrophobia. In *King Solomon's Mines* the heroes were shut
in: so, more terribly, the narrator imagined himself to be in
Poe's *Premature Burial*. Your breath shortens while you read it.
Now remember the chapter called 'Mr Bedford Alone' in H. G.
Wells's *First Men in the Moon*. There Bedford finds himself

shut out on the surface of the Moon just as the long lunar day is drawing to its close—and with the day go the air and all heat. Read it from the terrible moment when the first tiny snowflake startles him into a realization of his position down to the point at which he reaches the 'sphere' and is saved. Then ask yourself whether what you have been feeling is simply suspense. 'Over me, around me, closing in on me, embracing me ever nearer was the Eternal . . . the infinite and final Night of space.' That is the idea which has kept you enthralled. But if we were concerned only with the question whether Mr Bedford will live or freeze, that idea is quite beside the purpose. You can die of cold between Russian Poland and new Poland, just as well as by going to the Moon, and the pain will be equal. For the purpose of killing Mr Bedford 'the infinite and final Night of space' is almost entirely otiose: what is by cosmic standards an infinitesimal change of temperature is sufficient to kill a man and absolute zero can do no more. That airless outer darkness is important not for what it can do to Bedford but for what it does to us: to trouble us with Pascal's old fear of those eternal silences which have gnawed at so much religious faith and shattered so many humanistic hopes: to evoke with them and through them all our racial and childish memories of exclusion and desolation: to present, in fact, as an intuition one permanent aspect of human experience.

And here, I expect, we come to one of the differences between life and art. A man really in Bedford's position would probably not feel very acutely that sidereal loneliness. The immediate issue of death would drive the contemplative object out of his mind: he would have no interest in the many degrees of increasing cold lower than the one which made his survival impossible. That is one of the functions of art: to present what the narrow and desperately practical perspectives of real life exclude.

I have sometimes wondered whether the 'excitement' may not be an element actually hostile to the deeper imagination. In inferior romances, such as the American magazines of 'scientifiction' supply, we often come across a really suggestive idea.

But the author has no expedient for keeping the story on the move except that of putting his hero into violent danger. In the hurry and scurry of his escapes the poetry of the basic idea is lost. In a much milder degree I think this has happened to Wells himself in the *War of the Worlds*. What really matters in this story is the idea of being attacked by something utterly 'outside'. As in *Piers Plowman* destruction has come upon us 'from the planets'. If the Martian invaders are merely dangerous — if we once become mainly concerned with the fact that they can *kill* us—why, then, a burglar or a bacillus can do as much. The real nerve of the romance is laid bare when the hero first goes to look at the newly fallen projectile on Horsell Common. 'The yellowish-white metal that gleamed in the crack between the lid and the cylinder had an unfamiliar hue. *Extra-terrestrial* had no meaning for most of the onlookers.' But *extra-terrestrial* is the key word of the whole story. And in the later horrors, excellently as they are done, we lose the feeling of it. Similarly in the Poet Laureate's *Sard Harker* it is the journey across the Sierras that really matters. That the man who has heard that noise in the cañon—'He could not think what it was. It was not sorrowful nor joyful nor terrible. It was great and strange. It was like the rock speaking'—that this man should be later in danger of mere murder is almost an impertinence.

It is here that Homer shows his supreme excellence. The landing on Circe's island, the sight of the smoke going up from amidst those unexplored woods, the god meeting us ('the messenger, the slayer of Argus')—what an anti-climax if all these had been the prelude only to some ordinary risk of life and limb! But the peril that lurks here, the silent, painless, unendurable change into brutality, is worthy of the setting. Mr de la Mare too has surmounted the difficulty. The threat launched in the opening paragraphs of his best stories is seldom fulfilled in any identifiable event: still less is it dissipated. Our fears are never, in one sense, realized: yet we lay down the story feeling that they, and far more, were justified. But perhaps the most remarkable achievement in this kind is that of Mr David

Lindsay's *Voyage to Arcturus*. The experienced reader, noting
the threats and promises of the opening chapter, even while he
gratefully enjoys them, feels sure that they cannot be carried
out. He reflects that in stories of this kind the first chapter is
nearly always the best and reconciles himself to disappointment;
Tormance, when we reach it, he forbodes, will be less interesting than Tormance seen from the Earth. But never will he have
been more mistaken. Unaided by any special skill or even any
sound taste in language, the author leads us up a stair of un-
predictables. In each chapter we think we have found his final
position; each time we are utterly mistaken. He builds whole
worlds of imagery and passion, any one of which would have
served another writer for a whole book, only to pull each of
them to pieces and pour scorn on it. The physical dangers,
which are plentiful, here count for nothing: it is we ourselves
and the author who walk through a world of spiritual dangers
which makes them seem trivial. There is no recipe for writing
of this kind. But part of the secret is that the author (like Kafka)
is recording a lived dialectic. His Tormance is a region of the
spirit. He is the first writer to discover what 'other planets' are
really good for in fiction. No merely physical strangeness or
merely spatial distance will realize that idea of otherness which
is what we are always trying to grasp in a story about voyaging
through space: you must go into another dimension. To con-
struct plausible and moving 'other worlds' you must draw on
the only real 'other world' we know, that of the spirit.

Notice here the corollary. If some fatal progress of applied
science ever enables us in fact to reach the Moon, that real
journey will not at all satisfy the impulse which we now seek
to gratify by writing such stories. The real Moon, if you could
reach it and survive, would in a deep and deadly sense be just
like anywhere else. You would find cold, hunger, hardship, and
danger; and after the first few hours they would be *simply*
cold, hunger, hardship, and danger as you might have met them
on Earth. And death would be simply death among those
bleached craters as it is simply death in a nursing home at

Sheffield. No man would find an abiding strangeness on the Moon unless he were the sort of man who could find it in his own back garden. 'He who would bring home the wealth of the Indies must carry the wealth of the Indies with him.'

Good stories often introduce the marvellous or supernatural, and nothing about Story has been so often misunderstood as this. Thus, for example, Dr Johnson, if I remember rightly, thought that children liked stories of the marvellous because they were too ignorant to know that they were impossible. But children do not always like them, nor are those who like them always children; and to enjoy reading about fairies—much more about giants and dragons—it is not necessary to believe in them. Belief is at best irrelevant; it may be a positive disadvantage. Nor are the marvels in good Story ever mere arbitrary fictions stuck on to make the narrative more sensational. I happened to remark to a man who was sitting beside me at dinner the other night that I was reading Grimm in German of an evening but never bothered to look up a word I didn't know, 'so that it is often great fun' (I added) 'guessing what it was that the old woman gave to the prince which he afterwards lost in the wood'. 'And specially difficult in a fairy-tale,' said he, 'where everything is arbitrary and therefore the object might be anything at all.' His error was profound. The logic of a fairy-tale is as strict as that of a realistic novel, though different.

Does anyone believe that Kenneth Grahame made an arbitrary choice when he gave his principal character the form of a toad, or that a stag, a pigeon, a lion, would have done as well? The choice is based on the fact that the real toad's face has a grotesque resemblance to a certain kind of human face—a rather apoplectic face with a fatuous grin on it. This is, no doubt, an accident in the sense that all the lines which suggest the resemblance are really there for quite different biological reasons. The ludicrous quasi-human expression is therefore changeless: the toad cannot stop grinning because its 'grin' is not really a grin at all. Looking at the creature we thus see, isolated and fixed, an aspect of human vanity in its funniest and most pardonable form; following that hint Grahame creates Mr Toad—an ultra-Jonsonian 'humour'. And we bring back the wealth of the Indies; we have henceforward more amusement in, and kindness towards, a certain kind of vanity in real life.

But why should the characters be disguised as animals at all? The disguise is very thin, so thin that Grahame makes Mr Toad on one occasion 'comb the dry leaves out of his *hair*'. Yet it is quite indispensable. If you try to rewrite the book with all the characters humanized you are faced at the outset with a dilemma. Are they to be adults or children? You will find that they can be neither. They are like children in so far as they have no responsibilities, no struggle for existence, no domestic cares. Meals turn up; one does not even ask who cooked them. In Mr Badger's kitchen 'plates on the dresser grinned at pots on the shelf'. Who kept them clean? Where were they bought? How were they delivered in the Wild Wood? Mole is very snug in his subterranean home, but what was he living *on*? If he is a *rentier* where is the bank, what are his investments? The tables in his forecourt were 'marked with rings that hinted at beer mugs'. But where did he get the beer? In that way the life of all the characters is that of children for whom everything is provided and who take everything for granted. But in other ways it is the life of adults. They go where they like and do what they please, they arrange their own lives.

To that extent the book is a specimen of the most scandalous escapism: it paints a happiness under incompatible conditions—the sort of freedom we can have only in childhood and the sort we can have only in maturity—and conceals the contradiction by the further pretence that the characters are not human beings at all. The one absurdity helps to hide the other. It might be expected that such a book would unfit us for the harshness of reality and send us back to our daily lives unsettled and discontented. I do not find that it does so. The happiness which it presents to us is in fact full of the simplest and most attainable things—food, sleep, exercise, friendship, the face of nature, even (in a sense) religion. That 'simple but sustaining meal' of 'bacon and broad beans and a macaroni pudding' which Rat gave to his friends has, I doubt not, helped down many a real nursery dinner. And in the same way the whole story, paradoxically enough, strengthens our relish for real life. This excursion into the preposterous sends us back with renewed pleasure to the actual.

It is usual to speak in a playfully apologetic tone about one's adult enjoyment of what are called 'children's books'. I think the convention a silly one. No book is really worth reading at the age of ten which is not equally (and often far more) worth reading at the age of fifty—except, of course, books of information. The only imaginative works we ought to grow out of are those which it would have been better not to have read at all. A mature palate will probably not much care for *crème de menthe*: but it ought still to enjoy bread and butter and honey.

Another very large class of stories turns on fulfilled prophecies—the story of Oedipus, or *The Man who would be King*, or *The Hobbit*. In most of them the very steps taken to prevent the fulfilment of the prophecy actually bring it about. It is foretold that Oedipus will kill his father and marry his mother. In order to prevent this from happening he is exposed on the mountain: and that exposure, by leading to his rescue and thus to his life among strangers in ignorance of his real parentage, renders possible both the disasters. Such stories produce (at least in me) a feeling of awe, coupled with a certain sort of bewilderment such as one often feels in looking at a complex pattern of lines that pass over and under one another. One sees, yet does not quite see, the regularity. And is there not good occasion both for awe and bewilderment? We have just had set before our imagination something that has always baffled the intellect: we have *seen* how destiny and free will can be combined, even how free will is the *modus operandi* of destiny. The story does what no theorem can quite do. It may not be 'like real life' in the superficial sense: but it sets before us an image of what reality may well be like at some more central region.

It will be seen that throughout this essay I have taken my examples indiscriminately from books which critics would (quite rightly) place in very different categories—from American 'scientifiction' and Homer, from Sophocles and *Märchen*, from children's stories and the intensely sophisticated art of Mr de la Mare. This does not mean that I think them of real literary merit. But if I am right in thinking that there is another enjoyment in Story besides the excitement, then popular romance even on the lowest level becomes rather more important than we had supposed. When you see an immature or uneducated person devouring what seem to you merely sensational stories, can you be sure what kind of pleasure he is enjoying? It is, of course, no good asking *him*. If he were capable of analysing his own experience as the question requires him to do, he would be neither uneducated nor immature. But because he is inarticulate we must not give judgement against him. He may be seeking only the recurring tension of imagined anxiety. But he may also, I believe, be receiving certain profound experiences which are, for him, not acceptable in any other form.

Mr Roger Lancelyn Green, writing in *English* not long ago, remarked that the reading of Rider Haggard had been to many a sort of religious experience. To some people this will have seemed simply grotesque. I myself would strongly disagree with it if 'religious' is taken to mean 'Christian'. And even if we take it in a sub-Christian sense, it would have been safer to say that such people had first met in Haggard's romances elements which they would meet again in religious experience if they ever came to have any. But I think Mr Green is very much nearer the mark than those who assume that no one has ever read the romances except in order to be thrilled by hair-breadth escapes. If he had said simply that something which the educated receive from poetry can reach the masses through stories of adventure, and almost in no other way, then I think he would have been right. If so, nothing can be more disastrous than the view that the cinema can and should replace popular written fiction. The elements which it excludes are precisely those which give the untrained mind its only access to the imaginative world. There is death in the camera.

As I have admitted, it is very difficult to tell in any given case whether a story is piercing to the unliterary reader's deeper imagination or only exciting his emotions. You cannot tell even by reading the story for yourself. Its badness proves very little. The more imagination the reader has, being an untrained reader, the more he will do for himself. He will, at a mere hint from the author, flood wretched material with suggestion and never guess that he is himself chiefly making what he enjoys. The nearest we can come to a test is by asking whether he often *re-reads* the same story.

It is, of course, a good test for every reader of every kind of book. An unliterary man may be defined as one who reads books once only. There is hope for a man who has never read Malory or Boswell or *Tristram Shandy* or Shakespeare's *Sonnets*: but what can you do with a man who says he 'has read' them, meaning he has read them once, and thinks that this settles the matter? Yet I think the test has a special application to the matter in hand. For excitement, in the sense defined above, is just what must disappear from a second reading. You cannot, except at the first reading, be really curious about what happened. If you find that the reader of popular romance— however uneducated a reader, however bad the romances—goes back to his old favourites again and again, then you have pretty good evidence that they are to him a sort of poetry.

The re-reader is looking not for actual surprises (which can come only once) but for a certain surprisingness. The point has often been misunderstood. The man in Peacock thought that he had disposed of 'surprise' as an element in landscape gardening when he asked what happened if you walked through the garden for the second time. Wiseacre! In the only sense that matters the surprise works as well the twentieth time as the first. It is the *quality* of unexpectedness, not the *fact* that delights us. It is even better the second time. Knowing that the 'surprise' is coming we can now fully relish the fact that this path through the shrubbery doesn't *look* as if it were suddenly going to bring us out on the edge of the cliff. So in literature. We do not enjoy a story fully at the first reading. Not till the curiosity, the sheer narrative lust, has been given its sop and laid asleep, are we at leisure to savour the real beauties. Till then, it is like wasting great wine on a ravenous natural thirst which merely wants cold wetness. The children understand this well when they ask for the same story over and over again, and in the same words. They want to have again the 'surprise' of discovering that what seemed Little-Red-Riding-Hood's grandmother is really the wolf. It is better when you know it is coming: free from the shock of actual surprise you can attend better to the intrinsic surprisingness of the *peripeteia*.

I should like to be able to believe that I am here in a very small way contributing (for criticism does not always come later than practice) to the encouragement of a better school of prose story in England: of story that can mediate imaginative life to the masses while not being contemptible to the few. But perhaps this is not very likely. It must be admitted that the art of Story as I see it is a very difficult one. What its central difficulty is I have already hinted when I complained that in the *War of the Worlds* the idea that really matters becomes lost or blunted as the story gets under way. I must now add that there is a perpetual danger of this happening in all stories. To be stories at all they must be series of events: but it must be understood that this series—the *plot*, as we call it—is only really a net whereby to catch something else. The real theme may be, and perhaps usually is, something that has no sequence in it, something other than a process and much more like a state or quality. Giantship, otherness, the desolation of space, are examples that have crossed our path. The titles of some stories illustrate the point very well. *The Well at the World's End*—can a man write a story to that title? Can he find a series of events following one another in time which will really catch and fix and bring home to us all that we grasp at on merely hearing the six words? Can a man write a story on Atlantis—or is it better to leave the word to work on its own? And I must confess that the net very seldom does succeed in catching the bird. Morris in *The Well at the World's End* came near to success—quite near enough to make the book worth many readings. Yet, after all, the best moments of it come in the first half.

But it does sometimes succeed. In the works of the late E. R. Eddison it succeeds completely. You may like or dislike his invented worlds (I myself like that of *The Worm Ouroboros* and strongly dislike that of *Mistress of Mistresses*) but there is here no quarrel between the theme and the articulation of the story. Every episode, every speech, helps to incarnate what the author is imagining. You could spare none of them. It takes the whole story to build up that strange blend of renaissance luxury and northern hardness. The secret here is largely the style, and especially the style of the dialogue. These proud, reckless, amorous people create themselves and the whole atmosphere of their world chiefly by talking. Mr de la Mare also succeeds, partly by style and partly by never laying the cards on the table. Mr David Lindsay, however, succeeds while writing a style which is at times (to be frank) abominable. He succeeds because his real theme is, like the plot, sequential, a thing in time, or quasi-time: a passionate spiritual journey. Charles Williams had the same advantage, but I do not mention his stories much here because they are hardly pure story in the sense we are now considering. They are, despite their free use of the supernatural, much closer to the novel; a believed religion, detailed character drawing, and even social satire all come in. *The Hobbit* escapes the danger of degenerating into mere plot and excitement by a very curious shift of tone. As the humour and homeliness of the early chapters, the sheer 'Hobbitry', dies away we pass insensibly into the world of epic. It is as if the battle of Toad Hall had become a serious *heimsökn* and Badger had begun to talk like Njal. Thus we lose one theme but find another. We kill—but not the same fox.

It may be asked why anyone should be encouraged to write a form in which the means are apparently so often at war with the end. But I am hardly suggesting that anyone who can write great poetry should write stories instead. I am rather suggesting what those whose work will in any case be a romance should aim at. And I do not think it unimportant that good work in this kind, even work less than perfectly good, can come where poetry will never come.

Shall I be thought whimsical if, in conclusion, I suggest that this internal tension in the heart of every story between the theme and the plot constitutes, after all, its chief resemblance to life? If Story fails in that way does not life commit the same blunder? In real life, as in a story, something must happen. That is just the trouble. We grasp at a state and find only a succession of events in which the state is never quite embodied. The grand idea of finding Atlantis which stirs us in the first chapter of the adventure story is apt to be frittered away in mere excitement when the journey has once been begun. But so, in real life, the idea of adventure fades when the day-to-day details begin to happen. Nor is this merely because actual hardship and danger shoulder it aside. Other grand ideas—homecoming, reunion with a beloved—similarly elude our grasp. Suppose there is no disappointment; even so—well, you are here. But now, something must happen, and after that something else. All that happens may be delightful: but can any such series quite embody the sheer state of being which was what we wanted? If the author's plot is only a net, and usually an imperfect one, a net of time and event for catching what is not really a process at all, is life much more? I am not sure, on second thoughts, that the slow fading of the magic in *The Well at the World's End* is, after all, a blemish. It is an image of the truth. Art, indeed, may be expected to do what life cannot do: but so it has done. The bird has escaped us. But it was at least entangled in the net for several chapters. We saw it close and enjoyed the plumage. How many 'real lives' have nets that can do as much?

In life and art both, as it seems to me, we are always trying to catch in our net of successive moments something that is not successive. Whether in real life there is any doctor who can teach us how to do it, so that at last either the meshes will become fine enough to hold the bird, or we be so changed that we can throw our nets away and follow the bird to its own country, is not a question for this essay. But I think it is sometimes done—or very, very nearly done—in stories. I believe the effort to be well worth making.

ON THREE WAYS OF WRITING FOR CHILDREN

I think there are three ways in which those who write for children may approach their work; two good ways and one that is generally a bad way.

I came to know of the bad way quite recently and from two unconscious witnesses. One was a lady who sent me the MS of a story she had written in which a fairy placed at a child's disposal a wonderful gadget. I say 'gadget' because it was not a magic ring or hat or cloak or any such traditional matter. It was a machine, a thing of taps and handles and buttons you could press. You could press one and get an ice cream, another and get a live puppy, and so forth. I had to tell the author honestly that I didn't much care for that sort of thing. She replied, 'No more do I, it bores me to distraction. But it is what the modern child wants.' My other bit of evidence was this. In my own first story I had described at length what I thought a rather fine high tea given by a hospitable faun to the little girl who was my heroine. A man, who has children of his own, said, 'Ah, I see how you got to that. If you want to please grown-up readers you give them sex, so you thought to yourself, "That won't do for children, what shall I give them instead? I know! The little blighters like plenty of good eating."' In reality, however, I myself like eating and drinking. I put in what I would have liked to read when I was a child and what I still like reading now that I am in my fifties.

The lady in my first example, and the married man in my second, both conceived writing for children as a special department of 'giving the public what it wants'. Children are, of course, a special public and you find out what they want and give them that, however little you like it yourself.

On Three Ways of Writing for Children

The next way may seem at first to be very much the same, but I think the resemblance is superficial. This is the way of Lewis Carroll, Kenneth Grahame, and Tolkien. The printed story grows out of a story told to a particular child with the living voice and perhaps *ex tempore*. It resembles the first way because you are certainly trying to give that child what it wants. But then you are dealing with a concrete person, this child who, of course, differs from all other children. There is no question of 'children' conceived as a strange species whose habits you have 'made up' like an anthropologist or a commercial traveller. Nor, I suspect, would it be possible, thus face to face, to regale the child with things calculated to please it but regarded by yourself with indifference or contempt. The child, I am certain, would see through that. In any personal relation the two participants modify each other. You would become slightly different because you were talking to a child and the child would become slightly different because it was being talked to by an adult. A community, a composite personality, is created and out of that the story grows.

The third way, which is the only one I could ever use myself, consists in writing a children's story because a children's story is the best art-form for something you have to say: just as a composer might write a Dead March not because there was a public funeral in view but because certain musical ideas that had occurred to him went best into that form. This method could apply to other kinds of children's literature besides stories. I have been told that Arthur Mee never met a child and never wished to: it was, from his point of view, a bit of luck that boys liked reading what he liked writing. This anecdote may be untrue in fact but it illustrates my meaning.

Within the species 'children's story' the sub-species which happened to suit me is the fantasy or (in a loose sense of that word) the fairy tale. There are, of course, other sub-species. E. Nesbit's trilogy about the Bastable family is a very good specimen of another kind. It is a 'children's story' in the sense that children can and do read it: but it is also the only form in which E. Nesbit could have given us so much of the humours of childhood. It is true that the Bastable children appear, successfully treated from the adult point of view, in one of her grown-up novels, but they appear only for a moment. I do not think she would have kept it up. Sentimentality is so apt to creep in if we write at length about children as seen by their elders. And the reality of childhood, as we all experienced it, creeps out. For we all remember that our childhood, as lived, was immeasurably different from what our elders saw. Hence Sir Michael Sadler, when I asked his opinion about a certain new experimental school, replied, 'I never give an opinion on any of those experiments till the children have grown up and can tell us *what really happened*.' Thus the Bastable trilogy, however improbable many of its episodes may be, provides even adults, in one sense, with more realistic reading about children than they could find in most books addressed to adults. But also, conversely, it enables the children who read it to do something much more mature than they realize. For the whole book is a character study of Oswald, an unconsciously satiric self-portrait, which every intelligent child can fully appreciate: but no child would sit down to read a character study in any other form. There is another way in which children's stories mediate this psychological interest, but I will reserve that for later treatment.

In this short glance at the Bastable trilogy I think we have stumbled on a principle. Where the children's story is simply the right form for what the author has to say, then of course readers who want to hear that, will read the story or re-read it, at any age. I never met *The Wind in the Willows* or the Bastable books till I was in my late twenties, and I do not think I have enjoyed them any the less on that account. I am almost inclined to set it up as a canon that a children's story which is enjoyed only by children is a bad children's story. The good ones last. A waltz which you can like only when you are waltzing is a bad waltz.

This canon seems to me most obviously true of that particular type of children's story which is dearest to my own taste, the fantasy or fairy tale. Now the modern critical world uses 'adult' as a term of approval. It is hostile to what it calls 'nostalgia' and contemptuous of what it calls 'Peter Pantheism'. Hence a man who admits that dwarfs and giants and talking beasts and witches are still dear to him in his fifty-third year is now less likely to be praised for his perennial youth than scorned and pitied for arrested development. If I spend some little time defending myself against these charges, this is not so much because it matters greatly whether I am scorned and pitied as because the defence is germane to my whole view of the fairy tale and even of literature in general. My defence consists of three propositions.

1. I reply with a *tu quoque*. Critics who treat *adult* as a term of approval, instead of as a merely descriptive term, cannot be adult themselves. To be concerned about being grown up, to admire the grown up because it is grown up, to blush at the suspicion of being childish; these things are the marks of childhood and adolescence. And in childhood and adolescence they are, in moderation, healthy symptoms. Young things ought to want to grow. But to carry on into middle life or even into early manhood this concern about being adult is a mark of really arrested development. When I was ten, I read fairy tales in secret and would have been ashamed if I had been found doing so. Now that I am fifty I read them openly. When I became a man I put away childish things, including the fear of childishness and the desire to be very grown up.

2. The modern view seems to me to involve a false conception of growth. They accuse us of arrested development because we have not lost a taste we had in childhood. But surely arrested development consists not in refusing to lose old things but in failing to add new things? I now like hock, which I am sure I should not have liked as a child. But I still like lemon-squash. I call this growth or development because I have been enriched: where I formerly had only one pleasure, I now have two. But if I had to lose the taste for lemon-squash before I acquired

the taste for hock, that would not be growth but simple change. I now enjoy Tolstoy and Jane Austen and Trollope as well as fairy tales and I call that growth: if I had had to lose the fairy tales in order to acquire the novelists, I would not say that I had grown but only that I had changed. A tree grows because it adds rings: a train doesn't grow by leaving one station behind and puffing on to the next. In reality, the case is stronger and more complicated than this. I think my growth is just as apparent when I now read the fairy tales as when I read the novelists, for I now enjoy the fairy tales better than I did in childhood: being now able to put more in, of course I get more out. But I do not here stress that point. Even if it were merely a taste for grown-up literature added to an unchanged taste for children's literature, addition would still be entitled to the name 'growth', and the process of merely dropping one parcel when you pick up another would not. It is, of course, true that the process of growing does, incidentally and unfortunately, involve some more losses. But that is not the essence of growth, certainly not what makes growth admirable or desirable. If it were, if to drop parcels and to leave stations behind were the essence and virtue of growth, why should we stop at the adult? Why should not *senile* be equally a term of approval? Why are we not to be congratulated on losing our teeth and hair? Some critics seem to confuse growth with the cost of growth and also to wish to make that cost far higher than, in nature, it need be.

3. The whole association of fairy tale and fantasy with childhood is local and accidental. I hope everyone has read Tolkien's essay on Fairy Tales, which is perhaps the most important contribution to the subject that anyone has yet made. If so, you will know already that, in most places and times, the fairy tale has not been specially made for, nor exclusively enjoyed by, children. It has gravitated to the nursery when it became unfashionable in literary circles, just as unfashionable furniture gravitated to the nursery in Victorian houses. In fact, many children do not like this kind of book, just as many children do

not like horsehair sofas: and many adults do like it, just as many adults like rocking chairs. And those who do like it, whether young or old, probably like it for the same reason. And none of us can say with any certainty what that reason is. The two theories which are most often in my mind are those of Tolkien and of Jung.

According to Tolkien[1] the appeal of the fairy story lies in the fact that man there most fully exercises his function as a 'subcreator'; not, as they love to say now, making a 'comment upon life' but making, so far as possible, a subordinate world of his own. Since, in Tolkien's view, this is one of man's proper functions, delight naturally arises whenever it is successfully performed. For Jung, fairy tale liberates Archetypes which dwell in the collective unconscious, and when we read a good fairy tale we are obeying the old precept 'Know thyself'. I would venture to add to this my own theory, not indeed of the Kind as a whole, but of one feature in it: I mean, the presence of beings other than human which yet behave, in varying degrees, humanly: the giants and dwarfs and talking beasts. I believe these to be at least (for they may have many other sources of power and beauty) an admirable hieroglyphic which conveys psychology, types of character, more briefly than novelistic presentation and to readers whom novelistic presentation could not yet reach. Consider Mr Badger in *The Wind in the Willows*—that extraordinary amalgam of high rank, coarse manners, gruffness, shyness, and goodness. The child who has once met Mr Badger has ever afterwards, in its bones, a knowledge of humanity and of English social history which it could not get in any other way.

Of course as all children's literature is not fantastic, so all fantastic books need not be children's books. It is still possible, even in an age so ferociously anti-romantic as our own, to write fantastic stories for adults: though you will usually need to have made a name in some more fashionable kind of literature

[1] J. R. R. Tolkien, 'On Fairy–Stories', *Essays Presented to Charles Williams* (1947), p. 66 ff.

before anyone will publish them. But there may be an author who at a particular moment finds not only fantasy but fantasy-for-children the exactly right form for what he wants to say. The distinction is a fine one. His fantasies for children and his fantasies for adults will have very much more in common with one another than either has with the ordinary novel or with what is sometimes called 'the novel of child life'. Indeed the same readers will probably read both his fantastic 'juveniles' and his fantastic stories for adults. For I need not remind such an audience as this that the neat sorting-out of books into age-groups, so dear to publishers, has only a very sketchy relation with the habits of any real readers. Those of us who are blamed when old for reading childish books were blamed when children for reading books too old for us. No reader worth his salt trots along in obedience to a time-table. The distinction, then, is a fine one: and I am not quite sure what made me, in a particular year of my life, feel that not only a fairy tale, but a fairy tale addressed to children, was exactly what I must write—or burst. Partly, I think, that this form permits, or compels you to leave out things I wanted to leave out. It compels you to throw all the force of the book into what was done and said. It checks what a kind, but discerning critic called 'the expository demon' in me. It also imposes certain very fruitful necessities about length.

If I have allowed the fantastic type of children's story to run away with this discussion, that is because it is the kind I know and love best, not because I wish to condemn any other. But the patrons of the other kinds very frequently want to condemn it. About once every hundred years some wiseacre gets up and tries to banish the fairy tale. Perhaps I had better say a few words in its defence, as reading for children.

It is accused of giving children a false impression of the world they live in. But I think no literature that children could read gives them less of a false impression. I think what profess to be realistic stories for children are far more likely to deceive them. I never expected the real world to be like the fairy tales. I think that I did expect school to be like the school stories. The fantasies did not deceive me: the school stories did. All stories in which children have adventures and successes which are possible, in the sense that they do not break the laws of nature, but almost infinitely improbable, are in more danger than the fairy tales of raising false expectations.

Almost the same answer serves for the popular charge of escapism, though here the question is not so simple. Do fairy tales teach children to retreat into a world of wish-fulfilment— 'fantasy' in the technical psychological sense of the word— instead of facing the problems of the real world? Now it is here that the problem becomes subtle. Let us again lay the fairy tale side by side with the school story or any other story which is labelled a 'Boy's Book' or a 'Girl's Book', as distinct from a 'Children's Book'. There is no doubt that both arouse, and imaginatively satisfy, wishes. We long to go through the looking glass, to reach fairy land. We also long to be the immensely popular and successful schoolboy or schoolgirl, or the lucky boy or girl who discovers the spy's plot or rides the horse that none of the cowboys can manage. But the two longings are very different. The second, especially when directed on something so close as school life, is ravenous and deadly serious. Its fulfilment on the level of imagination is in very truth compensatory: we run to it from the disappointments and humiliations of the real world: it sends us back to the real world undivinely discontented. For it is all flattery to the ego. The pleasure consists in picturing oneself the object of admiration. The other longing, that for fairy land, is very different. In a sense a child does not long for fairy land as a boy longs to be the hero of the first eleven. Does anyone suppose that he really and prosaically longs for all the dangers and discomforts of a fairy tale?—really wants dragons in contemporary England? It is not so. It would be much truer to say that fairy land arouses a longing for he knows not what. It stirs and troubles him (to his life-long enrichment) with the dim sense of something beyond his reach and, far from dulling or emptying the actual world, gives it a new dimension of depth. He does not despise real woods because he has read of enchanted woods: the reading makes all real woods a little enchanted. This is a special kind of longing. The boy reading the school story of the type I have in mind desires success and is unhappy (once the book is over) because he can't get it: the boy reading the fairy tale desires and is happy in the very fact of desiring. For his mind has not been concentrated on himself, as it often is in the more realistic story.

I do not mean that school stories for boys and girls ought not to be written. I am only saying that they are far more liable to become 'fantasies' in the clinical sense than fantastic stories are. And this distinction holds for adult reading too. The dangerous fantasy is always superficially realistic. The real victim of wishful reverie does not batten on the *Odyssey, The Tempest,* or *The Worm Ouroboros*: he (or she) prefers stories about millionaires, irresistible beauties, posh hotels, palm beaches and bedroom scenes—things that really might happen, that ought to happen, that would have happened if the reader had had a fair chance. For, as I say, there are two kinds of longing. The one is an *askesis,* a spiritual exercise, and the other is a disease.

A far more serious attack on the fairy tale as children's literature comes from those who do not wish children to be frightened. I suffered too much from night-fears myself in childhood to undervalue this objection. I would not wish to heat the fires of that private hell for any child. On the other hand, none of my fears came from fairy tales. Giant insects were my specialty, with ghosts a bad second. I suppose the ghosts came directly or indirectly from stories, though certainly not from fairy stories, but I don't think the insects did. I don't know anything my parents could have done or left undone which would have saved me from the pincers, mandibles, and eyes of those many-legged abominations. And that, as so many people have pointed out, is the difficulty. We do not know what will or will not frighten a child in this particular way. I say 'in this particular way' for we must here make a distinction. Those who say that children must not be frightened may mean two things. They may mean (1) that we must not do anything likely to give the child those haunting, disabling, pathological fears against which ordinary courage is helpless: in fact, *phobias*. His mind must, if possible, be kept clear of things he can't bear to think of. Or they may mean (2) that we must try to keep out of his mind the knowledge that he is born into a world of death, violence, wounds, adventure, heroism and cowardice, good and evil. If they mean the first I agree with them: but not if they mean the second. The second would indeed be to give children a false impression and feed them on escapism in the bad sense. There is something ludicrous in the idea of so educating a generation which is born to the Ogpu and the atomic bomb. Since it is so likely that they will meet cruel enemies, let them at least have heard of brave knights and heroic courage. Otherwise you are making their destiny not brighter but darker. Nor do most of us find that violence and bloodshed, in a story, produce any haunting dread in the minds of children. As far as that goes, I side impenitently with the human race against the modern reformer. Let there be wicked kings and beheadings, battles and dungeons, giants and dragons, and let villains be soundly killed at the end of the book. Nothing will persuade me that this causes an ordinary child any kind or degree of fear beyond what it wants, and needs, to feel. For, of course, it wants to be a little frightened.

The other fears—the phobias—are a different matter. I do not believe one can control them by literary means. We seem to bring them into the world with us ready made. No doubt the particular image on which the child's terror is fixed can sometimes be traced to a book. But is that the source, or only the occasion, of the fear? If he had been spared that image, would not some other, quite unpredictable by you, have had the same effect? Chesterton has told us of a boy who was more afraid of the Albert Memorial than anything else in the world. I know a man whose great childhood terror was the India paper edition of the *Encyclopaedia Britannica*—for a reason I defy you to guess. And I think it possible that by confining your child to blameless stories of child life in which nothing at all alarming ever happens, you would fail to banish the terrors, and would succeed in banishing all that can ennoble them or make them endurable. For in the fairy tales, side by side with the terrible figures, we find the immemorial comforters and protectors, the radiant ones; and the terrible figures are not merely terrible, but sublime. It would be nice if no little boy in bed, hearing, or thinking he hears, a sound, were ever at all frightened. But if he is going to be frightened, I think it better that he should think of giants and dragons than merely of burglars. And I think St George, or any bright champion in armour, is a better comfort than the idea of the police.

I will even go further. If I could have escaped all my own night-fears at the price of never having known 'faerie', would I now be the gainer by that bargain? I am not speaking carelessly. The fears were very bad. But I think the price would have been too high.

But I have strayed far from my theme. This has been inevitable for, of the three methods, I know by experience only the third. I hope my title did not lead anyone to think that I was conceited enough to give you advice on how to write a story for children. There were two very good reasons for not doing that. One is that many people have written very much better stories than I, and I would rather learn about the art than set up to teach it. The other is that, in a certain sense, I have never exactly 'made' a story. With me the process is much more like bird-watching than like either talking or building. I see pictures. Some of these pictures have a common flavour, almost a common smell, which groups them together. Keep quiet and watch and they will begin joining themselves up. If you were very lucky (I have never been as lucky as all that) a whole set might join themselves so consistently that there you had a complete story: without doing anything yourself. But more often (in my experience always) there are gaps. Then at last you have to do some deliberate inventing, have to contrive reasons why these characters should be in these various places doing these various things. I have no idea whether this is the usual way of writing stories, still less whether it is the best. It is the only one I know: images always come first.

Before closing, I would like to return to what I said at the beginning. I rejected any approach which begins with the question 'What do modern children like?' I might be asked, 'Do you equally reject the approach which begins with the question "What do modern children need?"'—in other words, with the moral or didactic approach?' I think the answer is Yes. Not because I don't like stories to have a moral: certainly not because I think children dislike a moral. Rather because I feel sure that the question 'What do modern children need?' will not lead you to a good moral. If we ask that question we are assuming too superior an attitude. It would be better to ask 'What moral do I need?' for I think we can be sure that what does not concern us deeply will not deeply interest our readers, whatever their age. But it is better not to ask the question at all. Let the pictures tell you their own moral. For the moral inherent in them will rise from whatever spiritual roots you have succeeded in striking during the whole course of your life. But if they don't show you any moral, don't put one in. For the moral you put in is likely to be a platitude, or even a falsehood, skimmed from the surface of your consciousness. It is impertinent to offer the children that. For we have been told on high authority that in the moral sphere they are probably at least as wise as we. Anyone who *can* write a children's story without a moral, had better do so: that is, if he is going to write children's stories at all. The only moral that is of any value is that which arises inevitably from the whole cast of the author's mind.

Indeed everything in the story should arise from the whole cast of the author's mind. We must write for children out of those elements in our own imagination which we share with children: differing from our child readers not by any less, or less serious, interest in the things we handle, but by the fact that we have other interests which children would not share with us. The matter of our story should be a part of the habitual furniture of our minds. This, I fancy, has been so with all great writers for children, but it is not generally understood. A critic not long ago said in praise of a very serious fairy tale that the author's tongue 'never once got into his cheek'. But why on earth should it?—unless he had been eating a seed-cake. Nothing seems to me more fatal, for this art, than an idea that whatever we share with children is, in the privative sense, 'childish' and that whatever is childish is somehow comic. We must meet children as equals in that area of our nature where we are their equals. Our superiority consists partly in commanding other areas, and partly (which is more relevant) in the fact that we are better at telling stories than they are. The child as reader is neither to be patronized nor idolized: we talk to him as man to man. But the worst attitude of all would be the professional attitude which regards children in the lump as a sort of raw material which we have to handle. We must of course try to do them no harm: we may, under the Omnipotence, sometimes dare to hope that we may do them good. But only such good as involves treating them with respect. We must not imagine that we are Providence or Destiny. I will not say that a good story for children could never be written by someone in the Ministry of Education, for all things are possible. But I should lay very long odds against it.

Once in a hotel dining-room I said, rather too loudly, 'I loathe prunes.' 'So do I,' came an unexpected six-year-old voice from another table. Sympathy was instantaneous. Neither of us thought it funny. We both knew that prunes are far too nasty to be funny. That is the proper meeting between man and child as independent personalities. Of the far higher and more difficult relations between child and parent or child and teacher, I say nothing. An author, as a mere author, is outside all that. He is not even an uncle. He is a freeman and an equal, like the postman, the butcher, and the dog next door.

34

SOMETIMES FAIRY STORIES MAY SAY BEST WHAT'S TO BE SAID

In the sixteenth century when everyone was saying that poets (by which they meant all imaginative writers) ought 'to please and instruct', Tasso made a valuable distinction. He said that the poet, as poet, was concerned solely with pleasing. But then every poet was also a man and a citizen; in that capacity he ought to, and would wish to, make his work edifying as well as pleasing.

Now I do not want to stick very close to the renaissance ideas of 'pleasing' and 'instructing'. Before I could accept either term it might need so much redefining that what was left of it at the end would not be worth retaining. All I want to use is the distinction between the author as author and the author as man, citizen, or Christian. What this comes to for me is that there are usually two reasons for writing an imaginative work, which may be called Author's reason and the Man's. If only one of these is present, then, so far as I am concerned, the book will not be written. If the first is lacking, it can't; if the second is lacking, it shouldn't.

In the Author's mind there bubbles up every now and then the material for a story. For me it invariably begins with mental pictures. This ferment leads to nothing unless it is accompanied with the longing for a Form: verse or prose, short story, novel, play or what not. When these two things click you have the Author's impulse complete. It is now a thing inside him pawing to get out. He longs to see that bubbling stuff pouring into that Form as the housewife longs to see the new jam pouring into the clean jam jar. This nags him all day long and gets in the way of his work and his sleep and his meals. It's like being in love.

While the Author is in this state, the Man will of course have to criticize the proposed book from quite a different point of view. He will ask how the gratification of this impulse will fit in with all the other things he wants, and ought to do or be. Perhaps the whole thing is too frivolous and trivial (from the Man's point of view, not the Author's) to justify the time and pains it would involve. Perhaps it would be unedifying when it was done. Or else perhaps (at this point the Author cheers up) it looks like being 'good', not in a merely literary sense, but 'good' all around.

This may sound rather complicated but it is really very like what happens about other things. You are attracted by a girl; but is she the sort of girl you'd be wise, or right, to marry? You would like to have lobster for lunch; but does it agree with you and is it wicked to spend that amount of money on a meal? The Author's impulse is a desire (it is very like an itch), and of course, like every other desire, needs to be criticized by the whole Man.

Let me now apply this to my own fairy tales. Some people seem to think that I began by asking myself how I could say something about Christianity to children; then fixed on the fairy tale as an instrument; then collected information about child-psychology and decided what age group I'd write for; then drew up a list of basic Christian truths and hammered out 'allegories' to embody them. This is all pure moonshine. I couldn't write in that way at all. Everything began with images; a faun carrying an umbrella, a queen on a sledge, a magnificent lion. At first there wasn't even anything Christian about them; that element pushed itself in of its own accord. It was part of the bubbling.

Then came the Form. As these images sorted themselves into events (i.e., became a story) they seemed to demand no love interest and no close psychology. But the Form which excludes these things is the fairy tale. And the moment I thought of that I fell in love with the Form itself: its brevity, its severe restraints on description, its flexible traditionalism, its inflexible

36

hostility to all analysis, digression, reflections and 'gas'. I was now enamoured of it. Its very limitations of vocabulary became an attraction; as the hardness of the stone pleases the sculptor or the difficulty of the sonnet delights the sonneteer.

On that side (as Author) I wrote fairy tales because the Fairy Tale seemed the ideal Form for the stuff I had to say.

Then of course the Man in me began to have his turn. I thought I saw how stories of this kind could steal past a certain inhibition which had paralysed much of my own religion in childhood. Why did one find it so hard to feel as one was told one ought to feel about God or about the sufferings of Christ? I thought the chief reason was that one was told one ought to. An obligation to feel can freeze feelings. And reverence itself did harm. The whole subject was associated with lowered voices; almost as if it were something medical. But supposing that by casting all these things into an imaginary world, stripping them of their stained-glass and Sunday school associations, one could make them for the first time appear in their real potency? Could one not thus steal past those watchful dragons? I thought one could.

That was the Man's motive. But of course he could have done nothing if the Author had not been on the boil first.

You will notice that I have throughout spoken of Fairy Tales, not 'children's stories'. Professor J. R. R. Tolkien in *The Lord of the Rings*[1] has shown that the connection between fairy tales and children is not nearly so close as publishers and educationalists think. Many children don't like them and many adults do. The truth is, as he says, that they are now associated with children because they are out of fashion with adults; have in fact retired to the nursery as old furniture used to retire there, not because the children had begun to like it but because their elders had ceased to like it.

I was therefore writing 'for children' only in the sense that I excluded what I thought they would not like or understand;

[1] I think Lewis really meant Professor Tolkien's essay 'On Fairy-Stories' in *Essays Presented to Charles Williams* (1947), p. 58.

not in the sense of writing what I intended to be below adult attention. I may of course have been deceived, but the principle at least saves one from being patronizing. I never wrote down to anyone; and whether the opinion condemns or acquits my own work, it certainly is my opinion that a book worth reading only in childhood is not worth reading even then. The inhibitions which I hoped my stories would overcome in a child's mind may exist in a grown-up's mind too, and may perhaps be overcome by the same means.

The Fantastic or Mythical is a Mode available at all ages for some readers; for others, at none. At all ages, if it is well used by the author and meets the right reader, it has the same power: to generalize while remaining concrete, to present in palpable form not concepts or even experiences but whole classes of experience, and to throw off irrelevancies. But at its best it can do more; it can give us experiences we have never had and thus, instead of 'commenting on life', can add to it. I am speaking, of course, about the thing itself, not my own attempts at it.

'Juveniles', indeed! Am I to patronize sleep because children sleep sound? Or honey because children like it?

ON JUVENILE TASTES

Not long ago I saw in some periodical the statement that 'Children are a distinct race'. Something like this seems to be assumed today by many who write, and still more who criticize, what are called children's books or 'juveniles'. Children are regarded as being at any rate a distinct *literary* species, and the production of books that cater for their supposedly odd and alien taste has become an industry; almost a heavy one.

This theory does not seem to me to be borne out by the facts. For one thing, there is no literary taste common to all children. We find among them all the same types as among ourselves. Many of them, like many of us, never read when they can find any other entertainment. Some of them choose quiet, realistic, 'slice-of-life' books (say, *The Daisy Chain*) as some of us choose Trollope.

Some like fantasies and marvels, as some of us like the *Odyssey*, Boiardo, Ariosto, Spenser, or Mr Mervyn Peake. Some care for little but books of information, and so do some adults. Some of them, like some of us, are omnivorous. Silly children prefer success stories about school life as silly adults like success stories about grown-up life.

We can approach the matter in a different way by drawing up a list of books which, I am told, have been generally liked by the young. I suppose Aesop, *The Arabian Nights*, *Gulliver*, *Robinson Crusoe*, *Treasure Island*, *Peter Rabbit*, and *The Wind in the Willows* would be a reasonable choice. Only the last three were written for children, and those three are read with pleasure by many adults. I, who disliked *The Arabian Nights* as a child, dislike them still.

It may be argued against this that the enjoyment by children of some books intended for their elders does not in the least refute the doctrine that there is a specifically childish taste. They select (you may say) that minority of ordinary books which happens to suit them, as a foreigner in England may select those English dishes which come nearest to suiting his alien palate. And the specifically childish taste has been generally held to be that for the adventurous and the marvellous.

Now this, you may notice, implies that we are regarding as specifically childish a taste which in many, perhaps in most, times and places has been that of the whole human race. Those stories from Greek or Norse mythology, from Homer, from Spenser, or from folklore which children (but by no means all children) read with delight were once the delight of everyone.

Even the fairy tale *proprement dit* was not originally intended for children; it was told and enjoyed in (of all places) the court of Louis XIV. As Professor Tolkien has pointed out, it gravitated to the nursery when it went out of fashion among the grown-ups, just as old-fashioned furniture gravitated to the nursery. Even if all children and no adults now liked the marvellous—and neither is the case—we ought not to say that the peculiarity of children lies in their liking it. The peculiarity is that they *still* like it, even in the twentieth century.

It does not seem to me useful to say, 'What delighted the infancy of the species naturally still delights the infancy of the individual.' This involves a parallel between individual and species which we are in no position to draw. What age is Man? Is the race now in its childhood, its maturity, or its dotage? As we don't know at all exactly when it began, and have no notion when it will end, this seems a nonsense question. And who knows if it will ever be mature? Man may be killed in infancy.

Surely it would be less arrogant, and truer to the evidence, to say that the peculiarity of child readers is that they are not peculiar. It is we who are peculiar. Fashions in literary taste come and go among the adults, and every period has its own shibboleths. These, when good, do not improve the taste of children, and, when bad, do not corrupt it; for children read only to enjoy. Of course their limited vocabulary and general ignorance make some books unintelligible to them. But apart from that, juvenile taste is simply human taste, going on from age to age, silly with a universal silliness or wise with a universal wisdom, regardless of modes, movements, and literary revolutions.

This has one curious result. When the literary Establishment—the approved canon of taste—is so extremely jejune and narrow as it is today, much has to be addressed in the first instance to children if it is to get printed at all. Those who have a story to tell must appeal to the audience that still cares for story-telling.

The literary world of today is little interested in the narrative art as such; it is preoccupied with technical novelties and with 'ideas', by which it means not literary, but social or psychological, ideas. The ideas (in the literary sense) on which Miss Norton's *The Borrowers* or Mr White's *Mistress Masham's Repose* are built would not need to be embodied in 'juveniles' at most periods.

It follows that there are now two very different sorts of 'writers for children'. The wrong sort believe that children are 'a distinct race'. They carefully 'make up' the tastes of these odd creatures—like an anthropologist observing the habits of a savage tribe—or even the tastes of a clearly defined age-group within a particular social class within the 'distinct race'. They dish up not what they like themselves but what that race is supposed to like. Educational and moral, as well as commercial, motives may come in.

The right sort work from the common, universally human, ground they share with the children, and indeed with countless adults. They label their books 'For Children' because children are the only market now recognized for the books they, anyway, want to write.

IT ALL BEGAN WITH A PICTURE...

The Editor has asked me to tell you how I came to write *The Lion, the Witch and the Wardrobe*. I will try, but you must not believe all that authors tell you about how they wrote their books. This is not because they mean to tell lies. It is because a man writing a story is too excited about the story itself to sit back and notice how he is doing it. In fact, that might stop the works; just as, if you start thinking about how you tie your tie, the next thing is that you find you can't tie it. And afterwards, when the story is finished, he has forgotten a good deal of what writing it was like.

One thing I am sure of. All my seven Narnian books, and my three science fiction books, began with seeing pictures in my head. At first they were not a story, just pictures. The *Lion* all began with a picture of a Faun carrying an umbrella and parcels in a snowy wood. This picture had been in my mind since I was about sixteen. Then one day, when I was about forty, I said to myself: 'Let's try to make a story about it.'

At first I had very little idea how the story would go. But then suddenly Aslan came bounding into it. I think I had been having a good many dreams of lions about that time. Apart from that, I don't know where the Lion came from or why He came. But once He was there He pulled the whole story together, and soon He pulled the six other Narnian stories in after Him.

So you see that, in a sense, I know very little about how this story was born. That is, I don't know where the pictures came from. And I don't believe anyone knows exactly how he 'makes things up'. Making up is a very mysterious thing. When you 'have an idea' could you tell anyone exactly *how* you thought of it?

ON CRITICISM

I want to talk about the ways in which an author who is also a critic may improve himself as a critic by reading the criticism of his own work. But I must narrow my subject a little further. It used to be supposed that one of the functions of a critic was to help authors to write better. His praise and censure were supposed to show them where and how they had succeeded or failed, so that next time, having profited by the diagnosis, they might cure their faults and increase their virtues. That was what Pope had in mind when he said, 'Make use of every friend—and every foe.' But that is not at all what I want to discuss. In that way the author–critic might no doubt profit, as a critic, by reviews of his critical work. I am considering how he could profit, as a critic, by reviews of his non-critical works: his poems, plays, stories, or what not; what he can learn about the art of criticism by seeing it practised on himself; how he can become a better, or less bad, critic of other men's imaginative works from the treatment of his own imaginative works. For I am going to contend that when your own work is being criticized you are, in one sense, in a specially advantageous position for detecting the goodness or badness of the critique.

This may sound paradoxical, but of course all turns on my reservation, *in one sense*. There is of course another sense in which the author of a book is of all men least qualified to judge the reviews of it. Obviously he cannot judge their evaluation of it, because he is not impartial. And whether this leads him, naïvely, to hail all laudatory criticism as good and damn all unfavourable criticism as bad, or whether (which is just as likely) it leads him, in the effort against that obvious bias, to lean over backwards till he under-rates all who praise and admires all who censure him, it is equally a disturbing factor. Hence, if by criticism, you mean solely valuation, no man can judge critiques of his own work. In fact, however, most of what we call critical writing contains quite a lot of things besides evaluation. This is specially so both of reviews and of the criticism contained in literary history: for both these always should, and usually try to, inform their readers as well as direct their judgement. Now in so far as his reviewers do that, I contend that the author can see the defects and merits of their work better than anyone else. And if he is also a critic I think he can learn from them to avoid the one and emulate the other; how not to make about dead authors' books the same mistakes that have been made about his own.

I hope it will now be clear that in talking about what I think I have learned from my own critics I am not in any sense attempting what might be called an 'answer to critics'. That would, indeed, be quite incompatible with what I am actually doing. Some of the reviews I find most guilty of the critical vices I am going to mention were wholly favourable; one of the severest I ever had appeared to me wholly free from them. I expect every author has had the same experience. Authors no doubt suffer from self-love, but it need not always be voracious to the degree that abolishes all discrimination. I think fatuous praise from a manifest fool may hurt more than any depreciation.

One critical fault I must get out of the way at once because it forms no part of my real theme: I mean dishonesty. Strict honesty is not, so far as I can see, even envisaged as an ideal in the modern literary world. When I was a young, unknown writer on the eve of my first publication, a kind friend said to me, 'Will you have any difficulty about reviews? I could mention you to a few people. . . .' It is almost as if one said to an undergraduate on the eve of a Tripos, 'Do you know any of the examiners? I could put in a word for you.' Years later another man who had reviewed me with modest favour wrote to me (though a stranger) a letter in which he said that he had really thought much more highly of my book than the review showed: 'but of course,' he said, 'if I'd praised it any more the So-and-So would not have printed me at all.' Another time someone had attacked me in a paper called X. Then he wrote a book himself. The editor of X immediately offered it to me, of all people, to review. Probably he only wanted to set us both by the ears for the amusement of the public and the increase of his sales. But even if we take the more favourable possibility—if we assume that this editor had a sort of rough idea of what they call sportsmanship, and said, 'A has gone for B, it's only fair to let B have a go at A'—it is only too plain that he has no idea of honesty towards the public out of whom he makes his living. They are entitled, at the very least, to honest, that is, to impartial, unbiased criticism: and he cannot have thought that I was the most likely person to judge this book impartially. What is even more distressing is that whenever I tell this story someone replies—mildly, unemphatically—with the question, 'And did you?' This seems to me insulting, because I cannot see how an honest man could do anything but what I did: refuse the editor's highly improper proposal. Of course they didn't mean it as an insult. That is just the trouble. When a man assumes my knavery with the intention of insulting me, it may not matter much. He may only be angry. It is when he assumes it without the slightest notion that anyone could be offended, when he reveals thus lightly his ignorance that there ever were any standards by which it could be insulting, that a chasm seems to open at one's feet.

If I exclude this matter of honesty from my main subject it is not because I think it unimportant. I think it very important indeed. If there should ever come a time when honesty in reviewers is taken for granted, I think men will look back on the present state of affairs as we now look on countries or periods in which judges or examiners commonly take bribes. My reason for dismissing the matter briefly is that I want to talk about the things I hope I have learned from my own reviewers, and this is not one of them. I had been told long before I became an author that one mustn't tell lies (not even by *suppressio veri* and *suggestio falsi*) and that we mustn't take money for doing a thing and then secretly do something quite different. I may add before leaving the point that one mustn't judge these corrupt reviewers too harshly. Much is to be forgiven to a man in a corrupt profession at a corrupt period. The judge who takes bribes in a time or place where all take bribes may, no doubt, be blamed: but not so much as a judge who had done so in a healthier civilization.

I now turn to my main subject.

The first thing I have learned from my reviewers is, not the necessity (we would all grant that in principle) but the extreme rarity of conscientiousness in that preliminary work which all criticism should presuppose. I mean, of course, a careful reading of what one criticizes. This may seem too obvious to dwell on. I put it first precisely because it is so obvious and also because I hope it will illustrate my thesis that in certain ways (not of course in others) the author is not the worst, but the best, judge of his critics. Ignorant as he may be of his book's value, he is at least an expert on its content. When you have planned and written and re-written the thing and read it twice or more in proof, you do know what is in it better than anyone else. I don't mean 'what is in it' in any subtle or metaphorical sense (there may, in that sense, be 'nothing in it') but simply what words are, and are not, printed on those pages. Unless you have been often reviewed you will hardly believe how few reviewers have really done their Prep. And not only hostile reviewers. For them one has some sympathy. To have to read an author who affects one like a bad smell or a toothache is hard work. Who can wonder if a busy man skimps this disagreeable task in order to get on as soon as possible to the far more agreeable exercise of insult and denigration. Yet we examiners do wade through the dullest, most loathsome, most illegible answers before we give a mark; not because we like it, not even because we think the answer is worth it, but because this is the thing we have accepted pay for doing. In fact, however, laudatory critics often show an equal ignorance of the text. They too had rather write than read. Sometimes, in both sorts of review, the ignorance is not due to idleness. A great many people start by thinking they know what you will say, and honestly believe they have read what they expected to read. But for whatever reason, it is certainly the case that if you are often reviewed you will find yourself repeatedly blamed and praised for saying what you never said and for not saying what you have said.

Now of course it is true that a good critic may form a correct estimate of a book without reading every word of it. That perhaps is what Sidney Smith meant when he said 'You should never read a book before you review it. It will only prejudice you.' I am not, however, speaking of evaluations based on an imperfect reading, but of direct factual falsehoods about what it contains or does not contain. Negative statements are of course particularly dangerous for the lazy or hurried reviewer. And here, at once, is a lesson for us all as critics. One passage out of the whole *Faerie Queene* will justify you in saying that Spenser sometimes does so-and-so: only an exhaustive reading and an unerring memory will justify the statement that he never does so. This everyone sees. What more easily escapes one is the concealed negative in statements apparently positive: for example in any statement that contains the predicate 'new'. One says lightly that something which Donne or Sterne or Hopkins did was new: thus committing oneself to the negative that no one had done it before. But this is beyond one's knowledge; taken rigorously, it is beyond anyone's knowledge. Again, things we are all apt to say about the growth or development of a poet may often imply the negative that he wrote nothing except what has come down to us—which no one knows. We have not seen the contents of his waste paper basket. If we had, what now looks like an abrupt change in his manner from poem A to poem B might turn out not to have been abrupt at all.

It would be wrong to leave this point without saying that, however it may be with reviewers, academic critics seem to me now better than they ever were before. The days when Macaulay could get away with the idea that the *Faerie Queene* contained the death of the Blatant Beast, or Dryden with the remark that Chapman translated the *Iliad* in Alexandrines, are over. On the whole we now do our homework pretty well. But not yet perfectly. About the more obscure works ideas still circulate from one critic to another which have obviously not been verified by actual reading. I have an amusing piece of private evidence in my possession. My copy of a certain voluminous poet formerly belonged to a great scholar. At first I thought I had found a treasure. The first and second page were richly, and most learnedly annotated in a neat, legible hand. There were fewer on the third; after that, for the rest of the first poem, there was nothing. Each work was in the same state: the first few pages annotated, the rest in mint condition. 'Thus far into the bowels of the land' each time, and no further. Yet he had written on these works.

That, then, is the first lesson the reviewers taught me. There is, of course, another lesson in it. Let no one try to make a living by becoming a reviewer except as a last resource. This fatal ignorance of the text is not always the fruit of laziness or malice. It may be mere defeat by an intolerable burden. To live night and day with that hopeless mountain of new books (mostly uncongenial) piling up on your desk, to be compelled to say something where you have nothing to say, to be always behindhand—indeed much is to be excused to one so enslaved. But of course to say that a thing is excusable is to confess that it needs excuse.

I now turn to something which interests me much more because the bottom sin I detect in the reviewers is one which I believe we shall all find it very difficult to banish from our own critical work. Nearly all critics are prone to imagine that they know a great many facts relevant to a book which in reality they don't know. The author inevitably perceives their ignorance because he (often he alone) knows the real facts. This critical vice may take many different forms.

48

1. Nearly all reviewers assume that your books were written in the same order in which they were published and all shortly before publication. There was a very good instance of this lately in the reviews of Tolkien's *Lord of the Rings*. Most critics assumed (this illustrates a different vice) that it must be a political allegory and a good many thought that the master Ring must 'be' the atomic bomb. Anyone who knew the real history of the composition knew that this was not only erroneous, but impossible; chronologically impossible. Others assumed that the mythology of his romance had grown out of his children's story *The Hobbit*. This, again, he and his friends knew to be mainly false. Now of course nobody blames the critics for not knowing these things: how should they? The trouble is that they don't know they don't know. A guess leaps into their minds and they write it down without even noticing that it is a guess. Here certainly the warning to us all as critics is very clear and alarming. Critics of *Piers Plowman* and the *Faerie Queene* make gigantic constructions about the history of these compositions. Of course we should all admit such constructions to be conjectural. And as conjectures, you may ask, are they not, some of them, probable? Perhaps they are. But the experience of being reviewed has lowered my estimate of their probability. Because, when you start by knowing the facts, you find that the constructions are very often wholly wrong. Apparently the chances of their being right are low, even when they are made along quite sensible lines. Of course I am not forgetting that the reviewer has (quite rightly) devoted less study to my book than the scholar has devoted to Langland or Spenser. But I should have expected that to be compensated for by other advantages which he has and the scholar lacks. After all, he lives in the same period as I, subjected to the same currents of taste and opinion, and has undergone the same kind of education. He can hardly help knowing—reviewers are good at this sort of thing and take an interest in it—quite a lot about my generation, my period, and the circles in which I probably move. He and I may even have common acquaintances. Surely he is

at least as well placed for guessing about me as any scholar is for guessing about the dead. Yet he seldom guesses right. Hence I cannot resist the conviction that similar guesses about the dead seem plausible only because the dead are not there to refute them; that five minutes conversation with the real Spenser or the real Langland might blow the whole laborious fabric into smithereens. And notice that in all these conjectures the reviewer's error has been quite gratuitous. He has been neglecting the thing he is paid to do, and perhaps could do, in order to do something different. His business was to give information about the book and to pass judgement on it. These guesses about its history are quite beside the mark. And on this point, I feel pretty sure that I write without bias. The imaginary histories written about my books are by no means always offensive. Sometimes they are even complimentary. There is nothing against them except that they're not true, and would be rather irrelevant if they were. *Mutato nomine de me.* I must learn not to do the like about the dead: and if I hazard a conjecture, it must be with full knowledge, and with a clear warning to my readers, that it is a long shot, far more likely to be wrong than right.

2. Another type of critic who speculates about the genesis of your book is the amateur psychologist. He has a Freudian theory of literature and claims to know all about your inhibitions. He knows what unacknowledged wishes you were gratifying. And here of course one cannot, in the same sense as before, claim to start by knowing all the facts. By definition you are unconscious of the things he professes to discover. Therefore the more loudly you disclaim them, the more right he must be: though, oddly enough, if you admitted them, that would prove him right too. And there is a further difficulty: one is not here so free from bias, for this procedure is almost entirely confined to hostile reviewers. And now that I come to think of it, I have seldom seen it practised on a dead author except by a scholar who intended, in some measure, to debunk him. That in itself is perhaps significant. And it would not be unreasonable to

point out that the evidence on which such amateur psychologists base their diagnosis would not be thought sufficient by a professional. They have not had their author on the sofa, nor heard his dreams, and had the whole case-history. But I am here concerned only with what the author can say about such reviews solely because he is the author. And surely, however ignorant he is of his unconscious, he knows something more than they about the content of his conscious mind. And he will find them wholly overlooking the (to him) perfectly obvious conscious motive for some things. If they mentioned this and then discounted it as the author's (or patient's) 'rationalization', they might be right. But it is clear that they have never thought of it. They have never seen why, from the very structure of your story, from the very nature of story telling in general, that episode or image (or something like it) had to come in at that point. It is in fact quite clear that there is one impulse in your mind of which, with all their psychology, they have never reckoned: the plastic impulse, the impulse to make a thing, to shape, to give unity, relief, contrast, pattern. But this, unhappily, is the impulse which chiefly caused the book to be written at all. They have, clearly, no such impulse themselves, and they do not suspect it in others. They seem to fancy that a book trickles out of one like a sigh or a tear or automatic writing. It may well be that there is much in every book which comes from the unconscious. But when it is your own book you know the conscious motives as well. You may be wrong in thinking that these often give the full explanation of this or that. But you can hardly believe accounts of the sea-bottom given by those who are blind to the most obvious objects on the surface. They could be right only by accident. And I, if I attempt any similar diagnosis about the dead, shall equally be right, if at all, only by accident.

The truth is that a very large part of what comes up from the unconscious and which, for that very reason, seems so attractive and important in the early stages of planning a book, is weeded out and jettisoned long before the job is done: just as people (if they are not bores) tell us of their dreams only those which are amusing or in some other way interesting by the standards of the waking mind.

3. I now come to the imaginary history of the book's composition in a much subtler form. Here I think critics, and of course we when we criticize, are often deceived or confused as to what they are really doing. The deception may lurk in the words themselves. You and I might condemn a passage in a book for being 'laboured'. Do we mean by this that it sounds laboured? Or are we advancing the theory that it was in fact laboured? Or are we sometimes not quite sure which we mean? If we mean the second, notice that we are ceasing to write criticism. Instead of pointing out the faults in the passage we are inventing a story to explain, causally, how it came to have those faults. And if we are not careful we may complete our story and pass on as if we had done all that was necessary, without noticing that we have never even specified the faults at all. We explain something by causes without saying what the something is. We can do the same when we think we are praising. We may say that a passage is unforced or spontaneous. Do we mean that it sounds as if it were, or that it actually was written effortlessly and *currente calamo*? And whichever we mean, would it not be more interesting and more within the critics' province to point out, instead, those merits in the passage which made us want to praise it at all?

The trouble is that certain critical terms—*inspired, perfunctory, painstaking, conventional*—imply a supposed history of composition. The critical vice I am talking about consists in yielding to the temptation they hold out and then, instead of telling us what is good and bad in a book, inventing stories about the process which led to the goodness and badness. Or are they misled by the double sense of the word *Why*? For of course the question 'Why is this bad?' may mean two things: (*a*) What do you mean by calling it bad? Wherein does its badness consist? Give me the Formal Cause. (*b*) How did it become bad? Why did he write so ill? Give me the Efficient Cause. The first seems to me the essentially critical question. The critics I am thinking of answer the second, and usually answer it wrong, and unfortunately regard this as a substitute for the answer to the first.

Thus a critic will say of a passage, 'This is an afterthought.' He is just as likely to be wrong as right. He may be quite right in thinking it bad. And he must presumably think he has discerned in it the sort of badness which one might expect to occur in an afterthought. Surely an exposure of that badness itself would be far better than an hypothesis about its origin? Certainly this is the only thing that would make the critique at all useful to the author. I as author may know that the passage diagnosed as an afterthought was in reality the seed from which the whole book grew. I should very much like to be shown what inconsistency or irrelevance or flatness makes it look like an afterthought. It might help me to avoid these errors next time. Simply to know what the critic imagines, and imagines wrongly, about the history of the passage is of no use. Nor is it of much use to the public. They have every right to be told of the faults in my book. But this fault, as distinct from an hypothesis (boldly asserted as fact) about its origin, is just what they do not learn.

Here is an example which is specially important because I am quite sure the judgement which the critic was really making was correct. In a book of essays of mine the critic said that one essay was written without conviction, was task-work, or that my heart was not in it, or something like that. Now this in itself was plumb-wrong. Of all the pieces in the book it was the one I most cared about and wrote with most ardour.[1] Where the critic was right was in thinking it the worst. Everyone agrees with him about that. I agree with him. But you see that neither the public nor I learns anything about that badness from his criticism. He is like a doctor who makes no diagnosis and prescribes no cure but tells you how the patient got the disease (still

[1] Lewis, I am quite certain, is talking about the essay on William Morris in *Rehabilitations and Other Essays* (1939).

unspecified) and tells you wrong because he is describing scenes and events on which he has no evidence. The fond parents ask, 'What is it? Is it scarlatina or measles or chicken-pox?' The doctor replies, 'Depend upon it, he picked it up in one of those crowded trains.' (The patient actually has not travelled by train lately.) They then ask, 'But what are we to do? How are we to treat him?' The doctor replies, 'You may be quite sure it was an infection.' Then he climbs into his car and drives away.

Notice here again the total disregard of writing as a skill, the assumption that the writer's psychological state always flows unimpeded and undisguised into the product. How can they not know that in writing as in carpentry or tennis-playing or prayer or love-making or cookery or administration or anything else there is both skill and also those temporary heightenings and lowerings of skill which a man describes by saying that he is in good or bad form, that his hand is 'in' or 'out', that this is one of his good days or his bad days?

Such is the lesson, but it is very difficult to apply. It needs great perseverance to force oneself, in one's own criticism, to attend always to the product before one instead of writing fiction about the author's state of mind or methods of work: to which of course one has no direct access. 'Sincere', for example, is a word we should avoid. The real question is what makes a thing *sound* sincere or not. Anyone who has censored letters in the army must know that semi-literate people, though not in reality less sincere than others, very seldom *sound* sincere when they use the written word. Indeed we all know from our own experience in writing letters of condolence that the occasions on which we really feel most are not necessarily those on which our letters would suggest this. Another day, when we felt far less, our letter may have been more convincing. And of course the danger of error is greater in proportion as our own experience in the form we are criticizing is less. When we are criticizing a kind of work we have never attempted ourselves, we must realise that we do not know how such things are written and what is difficult or easy to do in them and how particular faults are likely to occur. Many critics quite clearly have an idea of how they think they would proceed if they tried to write the sort of book you have written, and assume that you were doing that. They often reveal unconsciously why they never have written a book of that kind.

I don't mean at all that we must never criticize work of a kind we have never done. On the contrary we must do nothing but criticize it. We may analyse and weigh its virtues and defects. What we must not do is to write imaginary histories. I know that all beer in railway refreshment rooms is bad and I could to some extent say 'why' (in one sense of the word: that is, I could give the Formal Cause)—it is tepid, sour, cloudy, and weak. But to tell you 'why' in the other sense (the Efficient Cause) I should need to have been a brewer or a publican or both and to know how beer should be brewed and kept and handled.

I would gladly be no more austere than is necessary. I must admit that words which seem, in their literal sense, to imply a history of the composition may sometimes be used as merely elliptical pointers to the character of the work done. When a man says that something is 'forced' or 'effortless' he may not really be claiming to know how it was written but only indicating in a kind of short-hand a quality he supposes everyone will recognize. And perhaps to banish all expression of this kind from our criticism would be a counsel of perfection. But I am increasingly convinced of their danger. If we use them at all, we must do so with extreme caution. We must make it quite clear to ourselves and to our readers that we do not know and are not pretending to know how things were written. Nor would it be relevant if we did. What sounds forced would be no better if it had been dashed off without pains; what sounds inspired, no worse if it had been arduously put together *invita Minerva*.

I now turn to interpretation. Here of course all critics, and we among them, will make mistakes. Such mistakes are far more venial than the sort I have been describing, for they are not gratuitous. The one sort arise when the critic writes fiction instead of criticism; the other, in the discharge of a proper

55

function. At least I assume that critics ought to interpret, ought to try to find out the meaning or intention of a book. When they fail the fault may lie with them or with the author or with both.

I have said vaguely 'meaning' or 'intention'. We shall have to give each word a fairly definite sense. It is the author who *intends*; the book *means*. The author's intention is that which, if it is realized, will in his eyes constitute success. If all or most readers, or such readers as he chiefly desires, laugh at a passage, and he is pleased with this result, then his intention was comic, or he intended to be comic. If he is disappointed and humiliated at it, then he intended to be grave, or his intention was serious. *Meaning* is a much more difficult term. It is simplest when used of an allegorical work. In the *Romance of the Rose* plucking the rosebud means enjoying the heroine. It is still fairly easy when used of a work with a conscious and definite 'lesson' in it. *Hard Times* means, among other things, that elementary state education is bosh; *Macbeth*, that your sin will find you out; *Waverley*, that solitude and abandonment to the imagination in youth render a man an easy prey to those who wish to exploit him; the *Aeneid*, that the *res Romana* rightly demands the sacrifice of private happiness. But we are already in deep waters, for of course each of these books means a good deal more. And what are we talking about when we talk, as we do, of the 'meaning' of *Twelfth Night*, *Wuthering Heights*, or *The Brothers Karamazov*? And especially when we differ and dispute as we do, about their real or true meaning? The nearest I have yet got to a definition is something like this: the meaning of a book is the series or system of emotions, reflections, and attitudes produced by reading it. But of course this product differs with different readers. The ideally false or wrong 'meaning' would be the product in the mind of the stupidest and least sensitive and most prejudiced reader after a single careless reading. The ideally true or right 'meaning' would be that shared (in some measure) by the largest number of the best readers after repeated and careful readings over several generations, different periods, nationalities, moods, degrees of alertness, private pre-occupations, states of health, spirits, and the like cancelling one another out when (this is an important reservation) they cannot be fused so as to enrich one another. (This happens when one's readings of a work at widely different periods of one's own life, influenced by the readings that reach us indirectly through the works of critics, all modify our present reading so as to improve it.) As for the many generations, we must add a limit. These serve to enrich the perception of the meaning only so long as the cultural tradition is not lost. There may come a break or change after which readers arise whose point of view is so alien that they might as well be interpreting a new work. Medieval readings of the *Aeneid* as an allegory and Ovid as a moralist, or modern readings of the *Parlement of Foules* which make the duck and goose its heroes, would be examples. To delay, even if we cannot permanently banish such interpretations, is a large part of the function of scholarly, as distinct from pure, criticism; so doctors labour to prolong life though they know they cannot make men immortal.

Of a book's meaning, in this sense, its author is not necessarily the best, and is never a perfect, judge. One of his intentions usually was that it should have a certain meaning: he cannot be sure that it has. He cannot even be sure that the meaning he intended it to have was in every way, or even at all, better than the meaning which readers find in it. Here, therefore, the critic has great freedom to range without fear of contradiction from the author's superior knowledge.

Where he seems to me most often to go wrong is in the hasty assumption of an allegorical sense; and as reviewers make this mistake about contemporary works, so, in my opinion, scholars now often make it about old ones. I would recommend to both, and I would try to observe in my own critical practice, these principles. First, that no story can be devised by the wit of man which cannot be interpreted allegorically by the wit of some other man. The Stoic interpretations of primitive mythology, the Christian interpretations of the Old Testament, the medieval interpretations of the classics, all prove this. Therefore (2) the mere fact that you *can* allegorize the work before you is of itself no proof that it is an allegory. Of course you can allegorize it. You can allegorize anything, whether in art or real life. I think we should here take a hint from the lawyers. A man is not tried at the assizes until there has been shown to be a *prima-facie* case against him. We ought not to proceed to allegorize any work until we have plainly set out the reasons for regarding it as an allegory at all.

[Lewis, apparently, did not finish this essay for at the foot of the existing manuscript are the words:]

As regards other attributions of intention

One's own preoccupations

Quellenforschung. *Achtung*—dates

ON SCIENCE FICTION

Sometimes a village or small town which we have known all our lives becomes the scene of a murder, a novel, or a centenary, and then for a few months everyone knows its name and crowds go to visit it. A like thing happens to one's private recreations. I had been walking, and reading Trollope, for years when I found myself suddenly overtaken, as if by a wave from behind, by a boom in Trollope and a short-lived craze for what was called hiking. And lately I have had the same sort of experience again. I had read fantastic fiction of all sorts ever since I could read, including, of course, the particular kind which Wells practised in his *Time Machine*, *First Men in the Moon* and others. Then, some fifteen or twenty years ago, I became aware of a bulge in the production of such stories. In America whole magazines began to be exclusively devoted to them. The execution was usually detestable; the conceptions, sometimes worthy of better treatment. About this time the name *scientifiction*, soon altered to *science fiction*, began to be common. Then, perhaps five or six years ago, the bulge still continuing and even increasing, there was an improvement: not that very bad stories ceased to be the majority, but that the good ones became better and more numerous. It was after this that the *genre* began to attract the attention (always, I think, contemptuous) of the literary weeklies. There seems, in fact, to be a double paradox in its history: it began to be popular when it least deserved popularity, and to excite critical contempt as soon as it ceased to be wholly contemptible.

Of the articles I have read on the subject (and I expect I have missed many) I do not find that I can make any use. For one thing, most were not very well informed. For another, many were by people who clearly hated the kind they wrote about. It is very dangerous to write about a kind you hate. Hatred obscures all distinctions. I don't like detective stories and therefore all detective stories look much alike to me: if I wrote about them I should therefore infallibly write drivel. Criticism of kinds, as distinct from criticism of works, cannot of course be avoided: I shall be driven to criticize one sub-species of science fiction myself. But it is, I think, the most subjective and least reliable type of criticism. Above all, it should not masquerade as criticism of individual works. Many reviews are useless because, while purporting to condemn the book, they only reveal the reviewer's dislike of the kind to which it belongs. Let bad tragedies be censured by those who love tragedy, and bad detective stories by those who love the detective story. Then we shall learn their real faults. Otherwise we shall find epics blamed for not being novels, farces for not being high comedies, novels by James for lacking the swift action of Smollett. Who wants to hear a particular claret abused by a fanatical teetotaller, or a particular woman by a confirmed misogynist?

Moreover, most of these articles were chiefly concerned to account for the bulge in the output and consumption of science fiction on sociological and psychological grounds. This is of course a perfectly legitimate attempt. But here as elsewhere those who hate the thing they are trying to explain are not perhaps those most likely to explain it. If you have never enjoyed a thing and do not know what it feels like to enjoy it, you will hardly know what sort of people go to it, in what moods, seeking what sort of gratification. And if you do not know what sort of people they are, you will be ill-equipped to find out what conditions have made them so. In this way, one may say of a kind not only (as Wordsworth says of the poet) that 'you must love it ere to you it will seem worthy of your love', but that you must at least have loved it once if you are even to warn others against it. Even if it is a vice to read science fiction, those who cannot understand the very temptation to that vice will not be likely to tell us anything of value about it. Just as I, for instance, who have no taste for cards, could not find anything very useful to say by way of warning against deep play. They will be like the frigid preaching chastity, misers warning us against prodigality, cowards denouncing rashness. And because, as I have said, hatred assimilates all the hated objects, it will make you assume that all the things lumped together as science fiction are of the same sort, and that the psychology of all those who like to read any of them is the same. That is likely to make the problem of explaining the bulge seem simpler than it really is.

I myself shall not attempt to explain it at all. I am not interested in the bulge. It is nothing to me whether a given work makes part of it or was written long before it occurred. The existence of the bulge cannot make the kind (or kinds) intrinsically better or worse; though of course bad specimens will occur most often within it.

I will now try to divide this species of narrative into its sub-species. I shall begin with that sub-species which I think radically bad, in order to get it out of our way.

In this sub-species the author leaps forward into an imagined future when planetary, sidereal, or even galactic travel has become common. Against this huge backcloth he then proceeds to develop an ordinary love-story, spy-story, wreck-story, or crime-story. This seems to me tasteless. Whatever in a work of art is not used, is doing harm. The faintly imagined, and sometimes strictly unimaginable, scene and properties, only blur the real theme and distract us from any interest it might have had. I presume that the authors of such stories are, so to speak, Displaced Persons—commercial authors who did not really want to write science fiction at all, but who availed themselves of its popularity by giving a veneer of science fiction to their normal kind of work. But we must distinguish. A leap into the future, a rapid assumption of all the changes which are feigned to have occurred, is a legitimate 'machine' if it enables the author to develop a story of real value which could not have been told (or not so economically) in any other way. Thus John Collier in *Tom's A-Cold* (1933) wants to write a story of heroic action among people themselves semi-barbarous but supported by the surviving tradition of a literate culture recently overthrown. He could, of course, find an historical situation suitable to his purpose, somewhere in the early Dark Ages. But that would involve all manner of archaeological details which would spoil his book if they were done perfunctorily and perhaps distract our interest if they were done well. He is therefore, on my view, fully justified in positing such a state of affairs in England after the destruction of our present civilization. That enables him (and us) to assume a familiar climate, flora, and fauna. He is not interested in the process whereby the change came about. That is all over before the curtain rises. This supposition is equivalent to the rules of his game: criticism applies only to the quality of his play. A much more frequent use of the leap into the future, in our time, is satiric or prophetic: the author criticizes tendencies in the present by imagining them carried out ('produced', as Euclid would say) to their logical limit. *Brave New World* and *Nineteen Eighty-Four* leap to our minds. I can see no objection to such a 'machine'. Nor do I see much use in discussing, as someone did, whether books that use it can be called 'novels' or not. That is merely a question of definition. You may define the novel either so as to exclude or so as to include them. The best definition is that which proves itself most convenient. And of course to devise a definition for the purpose of excluding either *The Waves* in one direction or *Brave New World* in another, and then blame them for being excluded, is foolery.

I am, then, condemning not all books which suppose a future widely different from the present, but those which do so without a good reason, which leap a thousand years to find plots and passions which they could have found at home.

Having condemned that sub-species, I am glad to turn to another which I believe to be legitimate, though I have not the slightest taste for it myself. If the former is the fiction of the Displaced Persons, this might be called the fiction of Engineers. It is written by people who are primarily interested in space-

travel, or in other undiscovered techniques, as real possibilities
in the actual universe. They give us in imaginative form their
guesses as to how the thing might be done. Jules Verne's *Twenty
Thousand Leagues Under the Sea* and Wells's *Land Ironclads*
were once specimens of this kind, though the coming of the
real submarine and the real tank has altered their original
interest. Arthur Clarke's *Prelude to Space* is another. I am
too uneducated scientifically to criticize such stories on the
mechanical side; and I am so completely out of sympathy with
the projects they anticipate that I am incapable of criticizing
them as stories. I am as blind to their appeal as a pacifist is to
Maldon and *Lepanto*, or an aristocratophobe (if I may coin the
word) to the *Arcadia*. But heaven forbid that I should regard
the limitations of my sympathy as anything save a red light
which warns me not to criticize at all. For all I know, these may
be very good stories in their own kind.

I think it useful to distinguish from these Engineers' Stories a
third sub-species where the interest is, in a sense, scientific, but
speculative. When we learn from the sciences the probable
nature of places or conditions which no human being has experienced, there is, in normal men, an impulse to attempt to
imagine them. Is any man such a dull clod that he can look at
the moon through a good telescope without asking himself
what it would be like to walk among those mountains under
that black, crowded sky? The scientists themselves, the moment
they go beyond purely mathematical statements, can hardly
avoid describing the facts in terms of their probable effect on
the senses of a human observer. Prolong this, and give, along
with that observer's sense experience, his probable emotions
and thoughts, and you at once have a rudimentary science
fiction. And of course men have been doing this for centuries.
What would Hades be like if you could go there alive? Homer
sends Odysseus there and gives his answer. Or again, what
would it be like at the Antipodes? (For this was a question of
the same sort so long as men believed that the torrid zone
rendered them forever inaccessible.) Dante takes you there: he

describes with all the gusto of the later scientifictionist how surprising it was to see the sun in such an unusual position. Better
still, what would it be like if you could get to the centre of the
earth? Dante tells you at the end of the *Inferno* where he and
Virgil, after climbing down from the shoulders to the waist of
Lucifer, find that they have to climb up from his waist to his
feet, because of course they have passed the centre of gravitation. It is a perfect science fiction effect. Thus again Athanasius
Kircher in his *Iter Extaticum Celeste* (1656) will take you to all
the planets and most of the stars, presenting as vividly as he can
what you would see and feel if this were possible. He, like
Dante, uses supernatural means of transport. In Wells's *First
Men in the Moon* we have means which are feigned to be natural.
What keeps his story within this sub-species, and distinguishes
it from those of the Engineers, is his choice of a quite impossible
composition called cavorite. This impossibility is of course a
merit, not a defect. A man of his ingenuity could easily have
thought up something more plausible. But the more plausible,
the worse. That would merely invite interest in actual possibilities
of reaching the Moon, an interest foreign to his story. Never
mind how they got there; we are imagining what it would be
like. The first glimpse of the unveiled airless sky, the lunar
landscape, the lunar levity, the incomparable solitude, then the
growing terror, finally the overwhelming approach of the lunar
night—it is for these things that the story (especially in its
original and shorter form) exists.

How anyone can think this form illegitimate or contemptible
passes my understanding. It may very well be convenient not
to call such things novels. If you prefer, call them a very special
form of novels. Either way, the conclusion will be much the
same: they are to be tried by their own rules. It is absurd to
condemn them because they do not often display any deep or
sensitive characterization. They oughtn't to. It is a fault if they
do. Wells's Cavor and Bedford have rather too much than too
little character. Every good writer knows that the more unusual
the scenes and events of his story are, the slighter, the more

ordinary, the more typical his persons should be. Hence Gulliver is a commonplace little man and Alice a commonplace little girl. If they had been more remarkable they would have wrecked their books. The Ancient Mariner himself is a very ordinary man. To tell how odd things struck odd people is to have an oddity too much: he who is to see strange sights must not himself be strange. He ought to be as nearly as possible Everyman or Anyman. Of course, we must not confuse slight or typical characterization with impossible or unconvincing characterization. Falsification of character will always spoil a story. But character can apparently be reduced, simplified, to almost any extent with wholly satisfactory results. The greater ballads are an instance.

Of course, a given reader may be (some readers seem to be) interested in nothing else in the world except detailed studies of complex human personalities. If so, he has a good reason for not reading those kinds of work which neither demand nor admit it. He has no reason for condemning them, and indeed no qualification for speaking of them at all. We must not allow the novel of manners to give laws to all literature: let it rule its own domain. We must not listen to Pope's maxim about the proper study of mankind. The proper study of man is everything. The proper study of man as artist is everything which gives a foothold to the imagination and the passions.

But while I think this sort of science fiction legitimate, and capable of great virtues, it is not a kind which can endure copious production. It is only the first visit to the Moon or to Mars that is, for this purpose, any good. After each has been discovered in one or two stories (and turned out to be different in each) it becomes difficult to suspend our disbelief in favour of subsequent stories. However good they were they would kill each other by becoming numerous.

My next sub-species is what I would call the Eschatological. It is about the future, but not in the same way as *Brave New World* or *The Sleeper Awakes*. They were political or social. This kind gives an imaginative vehicle to speculations about the ultimate destiny of our species. Examples are Wells's *Time Machine*, Olaf Stapledon's *Last and First Men*, or Arthur Clarke's *Childhood's End*. It is here that a definition of science fiction which separates it entirely from the novel becomes imperative. The form of *Last and First Men* is not novelistic at all. It is indeed in a new form—the pseudo history. The pace, the concern with broad, general movements, the tone, are all those of the historiographer, not the novelist. It was the right form for the theme. And since we are here diverging so widely from the novel, I myself would gladly include in this sub-species a work which is not even narrative, Geoffrey Dennis's *The End of the World* (1930). And I would certainly include, from J. B. S. Haldane's *Possible Worlds* (1927), the brilliant, though to my mind depraved, paper called 'The Last Judgement'.

Work of this kind gives expression to thoughts and emotions which I think it good that we should sometimes entertain. It is sobering and cathartic to remember, now and then, our collective smallness, our apparent isolation, the apparent indifference of nature, the slow biological, geological, and astronomical processes which may, in the long run, make many of our hopes (possibly some of our fears) ridiculous. If *memento mori* is sauce for the individual, I do not know why the species should be spared the taste of it. Stories of this kind may explain the hardly disguised political rancour which I thought I detected in one article on science fiction. The insinuation was that those who read or wrote it were probably Fascists. What lurks behind such a hint is, I suppose, something like this. If we were all on board ship and there was trouble among the stewards, I can just conceive their chief spokesman looking with disfavour on anyone who stole away from the fierce debates in the saloon or pantry to take a breather on deck. For up there, he would taste the salt, he would see the vastness of the water, he would remember that the ship had a whither and a whence. He would remember things like fog, storms, and ice. What had seemed, in the hot, lighted rooms down below to be merely the scene for a political crisis, would appear once more as a tiny egg-shell moving rapidly through an immense darkness over an element in which man cannot live. It would not necessarily change his convictions about the rights and wrongs of the dispute down below, but it would probably show them in a new light. It could hardly fail to remind him that the stewards were taking for granted hopes more momentous than that of a rise in pay, and the passengers forgetting dangers more serious than that of having to cook and serve their own meals. Stories of the sort I am describing are like that visit to the deck. They cool us. They are as refreshing as that passage in E. M. Forster where the man, looking at the monkeys, realizes that most of the inhabitants of India do not care how India is governed. Hence the uneasiness which they arouse in those who, for whatever reason, wish to keep us wholly imprisoned in the immediate conflict. That perhaps is why people are so ready with the charge of 'escape'. I never fully understood it till my friend Professor Tolkien asked me the very simple question, 'What class of men would you expect to be most preoccupied with, and most hostile to, the idea of escape?' and gave the obvious answer: jailers. The charge of Fascism is, to be sure, mere mud-flinging. Fascists, as well as Communists, are jailers; both would assure us that the proper study of prisoners is prison. But there is perhaps this truth behind it: that those who brood much on the remote past or future, or stare long at the night sky, are less likely than others to be ardent or orthodox partisans.

I turn at last to that sub-species in which alone I myself am greatly interested. It is best approached by reminding ourselves of a fact which every writer on the subject whom I have read completely ignores. Far the best of the American magazines bears the significant title *Fantasy and Science Fiction*. In it (as also in many other publications of the same type) you will find not only stories about space-travel but stories about gods, ghosts, ghouls, demons, fairies, monsters, etc. This gives us our clue. The last sub-species of science fiction represents simply an imaginative impulse as old as the human race working under the special conditions of our own time. It is not difficult to see why those who wish to visit strange regions in search of such beauty, awe, or terror as the actual world does not supply have increasingly been driven to other planets or other stars. It is the result of increasing geographical knowledge. The less known the real world is, the more plausibly your marvels can be located near at hand. As the area of knowledge spreads, you need to go further afield: like a man moving his house further and further out into the country as the new building estates catch him up. Thus in Grimm's *Märchen*, stories told by peasants in wooded country, you need only walk an hour's journey into the next forest to find a home for your witch or ogre. The author of *Beowulf* can put Grendel's lair in a place of which he himself says *Nis þaet feor heonon Mil-gemearces*. Homer, writing for a maritime people has to take Odysseus several days' journey by sea before he meets Circe, Calypso, the Cyclops, or the Sirens. Old Irish has a form called the *immram*, a voyage among islands. Arthurian romance, oddly at first sight, seems usually content with the old *Märchen* machine of a neighbouring forest. Chrétien and his successors knew a great deal of real geography. Perhaps the explanation is that these romances are chiefly written by Frenchmen about Britain, and Britain in the past. *Huon of Bordeaux* places Oberon in the East. Spenser invents a country not in our universe at all; Sidney goes to an imaginary past in Greece. By the eighteenth century we have to move well out into the country. Paltock and Swift take us to remote seas, Voltaire to America. Rider Haggard had to go to unexplored Africa or Tibet; Bulwer Lytton, to the depths of the Earth. It might have been predicted that stories of this kind would, sooner or later, have to leave Tellus altogether. We know now that where Haggard put She and Kôr we should really find groundnut schemes or Mau Mau.

In this kind of story the pseudo-scientific apparatus is to be taken simply as a 'machine' in the sense which that word bore for the Neo-Classical critics. The most superficial appearance of plausibility—the merest sop to our critical intellect—will do. I am inclined to think that frankly supernatural methods are best. I took a hero once to Mars in a space-ship, but when I knew better I had angels convey him to Venus. Nor need the strange worlds, when we get there, be at all strictly tied to scientific probabilities. It is their wonder, or beauty, or suggestiveness that matter. When I myself put canals on Mars I believe I already knew that better telescopes had dissipated that old optical delusion. The point was that they were part of the Martian myth as it already existed in the common mind.

The defence and analysis of this kind are, accordingly, no different from those of fantastic or mythopoeic literature in general. But here sub-species and sub-sub-species break out in baffling multitude. The impossible—or things so immensely improbable that they have, imaginatively, the same status as the impossible—can be used in literature for many different purposes. I cannot hope to do more than suggest a few main types: the subject still awaits its Aristotle.

It may represent the intellect, almost completely free from emotion, at play. The purest specimen would be Abbott's *Flatland*, though even here some emotion arises from the sense (which it inculcates) of our own limitations—the consciousness that our own human awareness of the world is arbitrary and contingent. Sometimes such play gives a pleasure analogous to that of the conceit. I have unluckily forgotten both the name and author of my best example: the story of a man who is enabled to travel into the future, because himself, in that future when he shall have discovered a method of time travel, comes back to himself in the present (then, of course, the past) and fetches him.[1] Less comic, but a more strenuous game, is the very fine working out of the logical consequences of time-travel in Charles Williams's *Many Dimensions*: where, however, this element is combined with many others.

Secondly, the impossible may be simply a postulate to liberate farcical consequences, as in 'F. Anstey's' *Brass Bottle*. The garunda-stone in his *Vice Versa* is not so pure an example; a

[1] Lewis is thinking, I believe, of Robert A. Heinlein's 'By His Bootstraps' in *Spectrum: A Science Fiction Anthology* (1961).

serious moral and, indeed, something not far from pathos, come in—perhaps against the author's wish.

Sometimes it is a postulate which liberates consequences very far from comic, and, when this is so, if the story is good it will usually point a moral: of itself, without any didactic manipulation by the author on the conscious level. Stevenson's *Dr Jekyll and Mr Hyde* would be an example. Another is Marc Brandel's *Cast the First Shadow*, where a man, long solitary, despised, and oppressed, because he had no shadow, at last meets a woman who shares his innocent defect, but later turns from her in disgust and indignation on finding that she has, in addition, the loathsome and unnatural property of having no reflection. Readers who do not write themselves often describe such stories as allegories, but I doubt if it is as allegories that they arise in the author's mind.

In all these the impossibility is, as I have said, a postulate, something to be granted before the story gets going. Within that frame we inhabit the known world and are as realistic as anyone else. But in the next type (and the last I shall deal with) the marvellous is in the grain of the whole work. We are, throughout, in another world. What makes that world valuable is not, of course, mere multiplication of the marvellous either for comic effect (as in *Baron Munchausen* and sometimes in Ariosto and Boiardo) or for mere astonishment (as, I think, in the worst of the *Arabian Nights* or in some children's stories), but its quality, its flavour. If good novels are comments on life, good stories of this sort (which are very much rarer) are actual additions to life; they give, like certain rare dreams, sensations we never had before, and enlarge our conception of the range of possible experience. Hence the difficulty of discussing them at all with those who refuse to be taken out of what they call 'real life'—which means, perhaps, the groove through some far wider area of possible experience to which our senses and our biological, social, or economic interests usually confine us—or, if taken, can see nothing outside it but aching boredom or sickening monstrosity. They shudder and ask to go home.

Specimens of this kind, at its best, will never be common. I would include parts of the *Odyssey*, the *Hymn to Aphrodite*, much of the *Kalevala* and *The Faerie Queene*, some of Malory (but none of Malory's best work) and more of *Huon*, parts of Novalis's *Heinrich von Ofterdingen*, *The Ancient Mariner* and *Christabel*, Beckford's *Vathek*, Morris's *Jason* and the *Prologue* (little else) of the *Earthly Paradise*, MacDonald's *Phantastes*, *Lilith*, and *The Golden Key*, Eddison's *Worm Ouroboros*, Tolkien's *Lord of the Rings*, and that shattering, intolerable, and irresistible work, David Lindsay's *Voyage to Arcturus*. Also Mervyn Peake's *Titus Groan*. Some of Ray Bradbury's stories perhaps make the grade. W. H. Hodgson's *The Night Land* would have made it in eminence from the unforgettable sombre splendour of the images it presents, if it were not disfigured by a sentimental and irrelevant erotic interest and by a foolish, and flat archaism of style. (I do not mean that all archaism is foolish, and have never seen the modern hatred of it cogently defended. If archaism succeeds in giving us the sense of having entered a remote world, it justifies itself. Whether it is correct by philological standards does not then matter a rap.)

I am not sure that anyone has satisfactorily explained the keen, lasting, and solemn pleasure which such stories can give. Jung, who went furthest, seems to me to produce as his explanation one more myth which affects us in the same way as the rest. Surely the analysis of water should not itself be wet? I shall not attempt to do what Jung failed to do. But I would like to draw attention to a neglected fact: the astonishing intensity of the dislike which some readers feel for the mythopoeic. I first found it out by accident. A lady (and, what makes the story more piquant, she herself was a Jungian psychologist by profession) had been talking about a dreariness which seemed to be creeping over her life, the drying up in her of the power to feel pleasure, the aridity of her mental landscape. Drawing a bow at a venture, I asked, 'Have you any taste for fantasies and fairy tales?' I shall never forget how her muscles tightened, her hands clenched themselves, her eyes started as if with horror, and her voice changed, as she hissed out, 'I *loathe* them.' Clearly we here have to do not with a critical opinion but with something like a phobia. And I have seen traces of it elsewhere, though never quite so violent. On the other side, I know from my own experience, that those who like the mythopoeic like it with almost equal intensity. The two phenomena, taken together, should at least dispose of the theory that it is something trivial. It would seem from the reactions it produces, that the mythopoeic is rather, for good or ill, a mode of imagination which does something to us at a deep level. If some seem to go to it in almost compulsive need, others seem to be in terror of what they may meet there. But that is of course only suspicion. What I feel far more sure of is the critical *caveat* which I propounded a while ago. Do not criticize what you have no taste for without great caution. And above all, do not ever criticize what you simply can't stand. I will lay all the cards on the table. I have long since discovered my own private *phobia*, the thing I can't bear in literature, the thing which makes me profoundly uncomfortable, is the representation of anything like a quasi love affair between two children. It embarrasses and nauseates me. But of course I regard this not as a charter to write slashing reviews of books in which the hated theme occurs, but as a warning not to pass judgement on them at all. For my reaction is unreasonable: such child-loves quite certainly occur in real life and I can give no reason why they should not be represented in art. If they touch the scar of some early *trauma* in me, that is my misfortune. And I would venture to advise all who are attempting to become critics to adopt the same principle. A violent and actually resentful reaction to all books of a certain kind, or to situations of a certain kind, is a danger signal. For I am convinced that good adverse criticism is the most difficult thing we have to do. I would advise everyone to begin it under the most favourable conditions: this is, where you thoroughly know and heartily like the thing the author is trying to do, and have enjoyed many books where it was done well. Then you will have some chance of really showing that he has failed and perhaps even of showing why. But if our real reaction to a book is 'Ugh! I just can't bear this sort of thing,' then I think we shall not be able to diagnose whatever real faults it has. We may labour to conceal our emotion, but we shall end in a welter of emotive, unanalysed, vogue-words—'arch', 'facetious', 'bogus', 'adolescent', 'immature' and the rest. When we really know what is wrong we need none of these.

A REPLY TO PROFESSOR HALDANE

Before attempting a reply to Professor Haldane's *Auld Hornie, F.R.S.*, in *The Modern Quarterly*, I had better note the one point of agreement between us. I think, from the Professor's complaint that my characters are 'like slugs in an experimental cage who get a cabbage if they turn right and an electric shock if they turn left', he suspects me of finding the sanctions of conduct in reward and punishment. His suspicion is erroneous. I share his detestation for any such view and his preference for Stoic or Confucian ethics. Although I believe in an omnipotent God I do not consider that His omnipotence could in itself create the least obligation to obey Him. In my romances the 'good' characters are in fact rewarded. That is because I consider a happy ending appropriate to the light, holiday kind of fiction I was attempting. The Professor has mistaken the 'poetic justice' of romance for an ethical theorem. I would go further. Detestation for any ethic which worships success is one of my chief reasons for disagreeing with most communists. In my experience they tend, when all else fails, to tell me that I ought to forward the revolution because 'it is bound to come'. One dissuaded me from my own position on the shockingly irrelevant ground that if I continued to hold it I should, in good time, be 'mown down'—argued, as a cancer might argue if it could talk, that he must be right because he could kill me. I gladly recognize the difference between Professor Haldane and such communists as that. I ask him, in return, to recognize the difference between my Christian ethics and those, say, of Paley. There are, on his side as well as on mine, Vichy-like vermin who define the right side as the side that is going to win. Let us put them out of the room before we begin talking.

A Reply to Professor Haldane

My chief criticism of the Professor's article is that, wishing to criticize my philosophy (if I may give it so big a name) he almost ignores the books in which I have attempted to set it out and concentrates on my romances. He was told in the preface to *That Hideous Strength* that the doctrines behind that romance could be found, stripped of their fictional masquerade, in *The Abolition of Man*. Why did he not go there to find them? The result of his method is unfortunate. As a philosophical critic the Professor would have been formidable and therefore useful. As a literary critic—though even there he cannot be dull—he keeps on missing the point. A good deal of my reply must therefore be concerned with removal of mere misunderstandings.

His attack resolves itself into three main charges. (1) That my science is usually wrong; (2) That I traduce scientists; (3) That on my view scientific planning 'can only lead to Hell' (and that therefore I am 'a most useful prop to the existing social order', dear to those who 'stand to lose by social changes' and reluctant, for bad motives, to speak out about usury).

(1) My science is usually wrong. Why, yes. So is the Professor's history. He tells us in *Possible Worlds* (1927) that 'five hundred years ago . . . it was not clear that celestial distances were so much greater than terrestrial'. But the astronomical textbook which the Middle Ages used, Ptolemy's *Almagest*, had clearly stated (I. v.) that in relation to the distance of the fixed stars the whole Earth must be treated as a mathematical point and had explained on what observations this conclusion was based. The doctrine was well known to King Alfred and even to the author of a 'popular' book like the *South English Legendary*. Again, in *Auld Hornie*, the Professor seems to think that Dante was exceptional in his views on gravitation and the rotundity of the Earth. But the most popular and orthodox authority whom Dante could have consulted, and who died a year or so before his birth, was Vincent of Beauvais. And in his *Speculum Naturale* (VII. vii.) we learn that if there were a hole right through the terrestrial globe (*terre globus*) and you dropped

75

a stone into that hole, it would come to rest at the centre. In other words, the Professor is about as good a historian as I am a scientist. The difference is that his false history is produced in works intended to be true, whereas my false science is produced in romances. I wanted to write about imaginary worlds. Now that the whole of our own planet has been explored other planets are the only place where you can put them. I needed for my purpose just enough popular astronomy to create in 'the common reader' a 'willing suspension of disbelief'. No one hopes, in such fantasies, to satisfy a real scientist, any more than the writer of a historical romance hopes to satisfy a real archaeologist. (Where the latter effort is seriously made, as in *Romola*, it usually spoils the book.) There is thus a great deal of scientific falsehood in my stories: some of it known to be false even by me when I wrote the books. The canals in Mars are there not because I believe in them but because they are part of the popular tradition; the astrological character of the planets for the same reason. The poet, Sidney says, is the only writer who never lies, because he alone never claims truth for his statements. Or, if 'poet' be too high a term to use in such a context, we can put it another way. The Professor has caught me carving a toy elephant and criticizes it as if my aim had been to teach zoology. But what I was after was not the elephant as known to science but our old friend Jumbo.

(2) I think Professor Haldane himself probably regarded his critique of my science as mere skirmishing; with his second charge (that I traduce scientists) we reach something more serious. And here, most unhappily, he concentrates on the wrong book—*That Hideous Strength*—missing the strong point of his own case. If any of my romances could be plausibly accused of being a libel on scientists it would be *Out of the Silent Planet*. It certainly is an attack, if not on scientists, yet on something which might be called 'scientism'—a certain outlook on the world which is causally connected with the popularization of the sciences, though it is much less common among real scientists than among their readers. It is, in a word,

the belief that the supreme moral end is the perpetuation of our own species, and that this is to be pursued even if, in the process of being fitted for survival, our species has to be stripped of all those things for which we value it—of pity, of happiness, and of freedom. I am not sure that you will find this belief formally asserted by any writer: such things creep in as assumed, and unstated, major premisses. But I thought I could feel its approach; in Shaw's *Back to Methuselah*, in Stapledon, and in Professor Haldane's 'Last Judgement' (in *Possible Worlds*). I had noted, of course, that the Professor dissociates his own ideal from that of his Venerites. He says that his own ideal is 'somewhere in between' them and a race 'absorbed in the pursuit of individual happiness'. The 'pursuit of individual happiness' is, I trust, intended to mean 'the pursuit by each individual of his own happiness at the expense of his neighbour's'. But it might also be taken to support the (to me meaningless) view that there is some other kind of happiness—that something other than an individual is capable of happiness or misery. I also suspected (was I wrong?) that the Professor's 'somewhere in between' came pretty near the Venerite end of the scale. It was against this outlook on life, this ethic, if you will, that I wrote my satiric fantasy, projecting in my Weston a buffoon-villain image of the 'metabiological' heresy. If anyone says that to make him a scientist was unfair, since the view I am attacking is not chiefly rampant among scientists, I might agree with him: though I think such a criticism would be over sensitive. The odd thing is that Professor Haldane thinks Weston 'recognisable as a scientist'. I am relieved, for I had doubts about him. If I were briefed to attack my own books I should have pointed out that though Weston, for the sake of the plot, has to be a physicist, his interests seem to be exclusively biological. I should also have asked whether it was credible that such a gas-bag could ever have invented a mouse-trap, let alone a space-ship. But then, I wanted farce as well as fantasy.

Perelandra, in so far as it does not merely continue its

predecessor, is mainly for my co-religionists. Its real theme would not interest Professor Haldane, I think, one way or the other. I will only point out that if he had noticed the very elaborate ritual in which the angels hand over the rule of that planet to the humans he might have realized that the 'angelocracy' pictured on Mars is, for me, a thing of the past: the Incarnation has made a difference. I do not mean that he can be expected to be interested in this view as such: but it might have saved us from at least one political red-herring.

That Hideous Strength he has almost completely misunderstood. The 'good' scientist is put in precisely to show that 'scientists' as such are not the target. To make the point clearer, he leaves my N.I.C.E. because he finds he was wrong in his original belief that 'it had something to do with science' (p. 83). To make it clearer yet, my principal character, the man almost irresistibly attracted by the N.I.C.E. is described (p. 226) as one whose 'education had been neither scientific nor classical— merely "Modern". The severities both of abstraction and of high human tradition had passed him by. . . . He was . . . a glib examinee in subjects that require no exact knowledge.' To make it doubly and trebly clear the rake's progress of Wither's mind is represented (p. 438) as philosophical, not scientific at all. Lest even this should not be enough, the hero (who is, by the way, to some extent a fancy portrait of a man I know, but not of me) is made to say that the sciences are 'good and innocent in themselves' (p. 248), though evil 'scientism' is creeping into them. And finally, what we are obviously up against throughout the story is not scientists but *officials*. If anyone ought to feel himself libelled by this book it is not the scientist but the civil servant: and, next to the civil servant, certain philosophers. Frost is the mouthpiece of Professor Waddington's ethical theories: by which I do not, of course, mean that Professor Waddington in real life is a man like Frost.

What, then, was I attacking? Firstly, a certain view about values: the attack will be found, undisguised, in *The Abolition of Man*. Secondly, I was saying, like St James and Professor

Haldane, that to be a friend of 'the World' is to be an enemy of God. The difference between us is that the Professor sees the 'World' purely in terms of those threats and those allurements which depend on money. I do not. The most 'worldly' society I have ever lived in is that of schoolboys: most worldly in the cruelty and arrogance of the strong, the toadyism and mutual treachery of the weak, and the unqualified snobbery of both. Nothing was so base that most members of the school prole-tariat would not do it, or suffer it, to win the favour of the school aristocracy: hardly any injustice too bad for the aristocracy to practice. But the class system did not in the least depend on the amount of anyone's pocket money. Who needs to care about money if most of the things he wants will be offered by cringing servility and the remainder can be taken by force? This lesson has remained with me all my life. That is one of the reasons why I cannot share Professor Haldane's exaltation at the banishment of Mammon from 'a sixth of our planet's surface'. I have already lived in a world from which Mammon was banished: it was the most wicked and miserable I have yet known. If Mammon were the only devil, it would be another matter. But where Mammon vacates the throne, how if Moloch takes his place? As Aristotle said, 'Men do not become tyrants in order to keep warm.' All men, of course, desire pleasure and safety. But all men also desire power and all men desire the mere sense of being 'in the know' or the 'inner ring', of not be-ing 'outsiders': a passion insufficiently studied and the chief theme of my story. When the state of society is such that money is the passport to all these prizes, then of course money will be the prime temptation. But when the passport changes, the desires will remain. And there are many other possible passports: position in an official hierarchy, for instance. Even now, the ambitious and worldly man would not inevitably choose the post with the higher salary. The pleasure of being 'high up and far within' may be worth the sacrifice of some income.

(3) Thirdly, was I attacking scientific planning? According to Professor Haldane 'Mr Lewis's idea is clear enough. The

application of science to human affairs can only lead to Hell.'
There is certainly no warrant for 'can only'; but he is justified
in assuming that unless I had thought I saw a serious and
widespread danger I would not have given planning so central
a place even in what I called 'a fairy tale' and a 'tall story'. But
if you must reduce the romance to a proposition, the proposition would be almost the converse of that which the Professor
supposes: not 'scientific planning will certainly lead to Hell',
but 'Under modern conditions any effective invitation to Hell
will certainly appear in the guise of scientific planning'—as
Hitler's régime in fact did. Every tyrant must begin by claiming
to have what his victims respect and to give what they want. The
majority in most modern countries respect science and want
to be planned. And, therefore, almost by definition, if any man
or group wishes to enslave us it will of course describe itself
as 'scientific planned democracy'. It may be true that any real
salvation must equally, though by hypothesis truthfully, describe itself as 'scientific planned democracy'. All the more
reason to look very carefully at anything which bears that
label.

My fears of such a tyranny will seem to the Professor either
insincere or pusillanimous. For him the danger is all in the
opposite direction, in the chaotic selfishness of individualism.
I must try to explain why I fear more the disciplined cruelty of
some ideological oligarchy. The Professor has his own explanation of this; he thinks I am unconsciously motivated by the
fact that I 'stand to lose by social change'. And indeed it would
be hard for me to welcome a change which might well consign
me to a concentration camp. I might add that it would be like-
wise easy for the Professor to welcome a change which might
place him in the highest rank of an omnicompetent oligarchy.
That is why the motive game is so uninteresting. Each side can
go on playing *ad nauseam*, but when all the mud has been flung
every man's views still remain to be considered on their merits.
I decline the motive game and resume the discussion. I do not
hope to make Professor Haldane agree with me. But I should

like him at least to understand why I think devil worship a real possibility.

I am a democrat. Professor Haldane thinks I am not, but he bases his opinion on a passage in *Out of the Silent Planet* where I am discussing, not the relations of a species to itself (politics) but the relations of one species to another. His interpretation, if consistently worked out, would attribute to me the doctrine that horses are fit for an equine monarchy though not for an equine democracy. Here, as so often, what I was really saying was something which the Professor, had he understood it, would have found simply uninteresting.

I am a democrat because I believe that no man or group of men is good enough to be trusted with uncontrolled power over others. And the higher the pretentions of such power, the more dangerous I think it both to the rulers and to the subjects. Hence Theocracy is the worst of all governments. If we must have a tyrant a robber baron is far better than an inquisitor. The baron's cruelty may sometimes sleep, his cupidity at some point be sated; and since he dimly knows he is doing wrong he may possibly repent. But the inquisitor who mistakes his own cruelty and lust of power and fear for the voice of Heaven will torment us infinitely because he torments us with the approval of his own conscience and his better impulses appear to him as temptations. And since Theocracy is the worst, the nearer any government approaches to Theocracy the worse it will be. A metaphysic, held by the rulers with the force of a religion, is a bad sign. It forbids them, like the inquisitor, to admit any grain of truth or good in their opponents, it abrogates the ordinary rules of morality, and it gives a seemingly high, super-personal sanction to all the very ordinary human passions by which, like other men, the rulers will frequently be actuated. In a word, it forbids wholesome doubt. A political programme can never in reality be more than probably right. We never know all the facts about the present and we can only guess the future. To attach to a party programme—whose highest real claim is to reasonable prudence—the sort of assent which we should reserve for demonstrable theorems, is a kind of intoxication.

This false certainty comes out in Professor Haldane's article. He simply cannot believe that a man could really be in doubt about usury. I have no objection to his thinking me wrong. What shocks me is his instantaneous assumption that the question is so simple that there could be no real hesitation about it. It is breaking Aristotle's canon—to demand in every enquiry that degree of certainty which the subject matter allows. And not *on your life* to pretend that you see further than you do.

Being a democrat, I am opposed to all very drastic and sudden changes of society (in whatever direction) because they never in fact take place except by a particular technique. That technique involves the seizure of power by a small, highly disciplined group of people; the terror and the secret police follow, it would seem, automatically. I do not think any group good enough to have such power. They are men of like passions with ourselves. The secrecy and discipline of their organisation will have already inflamed in them that passion for the inner ring which I think at least as corrupting as avarice; and their high ideological pretensions will have lent all their passions the dangerous prestige of the Cause. Hence, in whatever direction the change is made, it is for me damned by its *modus operandi*. The worst of all public dangers is the committee of public safety. The character in *That Hideous Strength* whom the Professor never mentions is Miss Hardcastle, the chief of the secret police. She is the common factor in all revolutions; and, as she says, you won't get anyone to do her job well unless they get some kick out of it.

I must, of course, admit that the actual state of affairs may sometimes be so bad that a man is tempted to risk change even by revolutionary methods; to say that desperate diseases require desperate remedies and that necessity knows no law. But to yield to this temptation is, I think, fatal. It is under that pretext that every abomination enters. Hitler, the Machiavellian Prince, the Inquisition, the Witch Doctor, all claimed to be necessary.

A Reply to Professor Haldane

From this point of view is it impossible that the Professor could come to understand what I mean by devil worship, as a symbol? For me it is not merely a symbol. Its relation to the reality is more complicated, and it would not interest Professor Haldane. But it is at least partly symbolical and I will try to give the Professor such an account of my meaning as can be grasped without introducing the supernatural. I have to begin by correcting a rather curious misunderstanding. When we accuse people of devil worship we do not usually mean that they knowingly worship the devil. That, I agree, is a rare perversion. When a rationalist accuses certain Christians, say, the seventeenth-century Calvinists, of devil worship, he does not mean that they worshipped a being whom they regarded as the devil; he means that they worshipped as God a being whose character the rationalist thinks diabolical. It is clearly in that sense, and that sense only, that my Frost worships devils. He adores the 'macrobes' because they are beings stronger, and therefore to him 'higher', than men: worships them, in fact, on the same grounds on which my communist friend would have me favour the revolution. No man at present is (probably) doing what I represent Frost as doing: but he is the ideal point at which certain lines of tendency already observable will meet if produced.

The first of these tendencies is the growing exaltation of the collective and the growing indifference to persons. The philosophical sources are probably in Rousseau and Hegel, but the general character of modern life with its huge impersonal organisations may be more potent than any philosophy. Professor Haldane himself illustrates the present state of mind very well. He thinks that if one were inventing a language for 'sinless beings who loved their neighbours as themselves' it would be appropriate to have no words for 'my', 'I', and 'other personal pronouns and inflexions'. In other words he sees no difference between two opposite solutions of the problem of selfishness: between love (which is a relation between persons) and the abolition of persons. Nothing but a *Thou* can be loved and a *Thou* can exist only for an *I*. A society in which no one was conscious of himself as a person over against other persons, where none could say 'I love you', would, indeed, be free from selfishness, but not through love. It would be 'unselfish' as a bucket of water is unselfish. Another good example comes in *Back to Methuselah*. There, as soon as Eve has learned that generation is possible, she says to Adam, 'You may die when I have made a new Adam. Not before. But then, as soon as you like.' The individual does not matter. And therefore when we really get going (shreds of an earlier ethic still cling to most minds) it will not matter what you do to an individual.

Secondly, we have the emergence of 'the Party' in the modern sense—the Fascists, Nazis or Communists. What distinguishes this from the political parties of the nineteenth century is the belief of its members that they are not merely trying to carry out a programme but are obeying an impersonal force: that Nature, or Evolution, or the Dialectic, or the Race, is carrying them on. This tends to be accompanied by two beliefs which cannot, so far as I see, be reconciled in logic but which blend very easily on the emotional level: the belief that the process which the Party embodies is inevitable, and the belief that the forwarding of this process is the supreme duty and abrogates all ordinary moral laws. In this state of mind men can become devil-worshippers in the sense that they can now *honour*, as well as obey, their own vices. All men at times obey their vices: but it is when cruelty, envy, and lust of power appear as the commands of a great super-personal force that they can be exercised with self-approval. The first symptom is in language. When to 'kill' becomes to 'liquidate' the process has begun. The pseudo-scientific word disinfects the thing of blood and tears, or pity and shame, and mercy itself can be regarded as a sort of untidiness.

[Lewis goes on to say: 'It is, at present, in their sense of serving a metaphysical force that the modern "Parties" approximate most closely to religions. Odinism in Germany, or the cult of Lenin's corpse in Russia are probably less important but there is quite a . . . '—and here the manuscript ends. One page (I think no more) is missing. It was probably lost soon after the essay was written, and without Lewis's knowledge, for he had, characteristically, folded the manuscript and scribbled the title 'Anti-Haldane' on one side with a pencil.]

UNREAL ESTATES

This informal conversation between Professor Lewis, Kingsley Amis, and Brian Aldiss was recorded on tape in Professor Lewis's rooms in Magdalene College a short while before illness forced him to retire. When drinks are poured, the discussion begins——

ALDISS: One thing that the three of us have in common is that we have all had stories published in the *Magazine of Fantasy and Science Fiction*, some of them pretty far-flung stories. I take it we would all agree that one of the attractions of science fiction is that it takes us to unknown places.

AMIS: Swift, if he were writing today, would have to take us out to the planets, wouldn't he? Now that most of our *terra incognita* is—real estate.

ALDISS: There is a lot of the eighteenth century equivalent of science fiction which is placed in Australia or similar unreal estates.

LEWIS: Exactly: Peter Wilkins and all that. By the way, is anyone ever going to do a translation of Kepler's *Somnium*?

AMIS: Groff Conklin told me he had read the book; I think it must exist in translation. But may we talk about the worlds you created? You chose the science fiction medium because you wanted to go to strange places? I remember with respectful and amused admiration your account of the space drive in *Out of the Silent Planet*. When Ransom and his friend get into the spaceship he says, 'How does this ship work?' and the man says, 'It operates by using some of the lesser known properties of——' what was it?

LEWIS: Solar radiation. Ransom was reporting words without a meaning to him, which is what a layman gets when he
asks for a scientific explanation. Obviously it was vague,
because I'm no scientist and not interested in the purely
technical side of it.

ALDISS: It's almost a quarter of a century since you wrote
that first novel of the trilogy.

LEWIS: Have I been a prophet?

ALDISS: You have to a certain extent; at least, the idea of
vessels propelled by solar radiation is back in favour
again. Cordwiner Smith used it poetically, James Blish
tried to use it technically in *The Star Dwellers*.

LEWIS: In my case it was pure mumbo-jumbo, and perhaps
meant primarily to convince me.

AMIS: Obviously when one deals with isolated planets or isolated islands one does this for a certain purpose. A setting
in contemporary London or a London of the future
couldn't provide one with the same isolation and the
heightening of consciousness it engenders.

LEWIS: The starting point of the second novel, *Perelandra*,
was my mental picture of the floating islands. The whole
of the rest of my labours in a sense consisted of building up
a world in which floating islands could exist. And then of
course the story about an averted fall developed. This is
because, as you know, having got your people to this exciting country, something must happen.

AMIS: That frequently taxes people very much.

ALDISS: But I am surprised that you put it this way round. I
would have thought that you constructed *Perelandra* for
the didactic purpose.

LEWIS: Yes, everyone thinks that. They are quite wrong.

AMIS: If I may say a word on Professor Lewis's side, there
was a didactic purpose of course; a lot of very interesting
profound things were said, but—correct me if I'm wrong—
I'd have thought a simple sense of wonder, extraordinary
things going on, were the motive forces behind the creation.

LEWIS: Quite, but something has got to happen. The story of this averted fall came in very conveniently. Of course it wouldn't have been that particular story if I wasn't interested in those particular ideas on other grounds. But that isn't what I started from. I've never started from a message or a moral, have you?

AMIS: No, never. You get interested in the situation.

LEWIS: The story itself should force its moral upon you. You find out what the moral is by writing the story.

AMIS: Exactly: I think that sort of thing is true of all kinds of fiction.

ALDISS: But a lot of science fiction has been written from the other point of view: those dreary sociological dramas that appear from time to time, started with a didactic purpose—to make a preconceived point—and they've got no further.

LEWIS: I suppose Gulliver started from a straight point of view? Or did it really start because he wanted to write about a lot of big and little men?

AMIS: Possibly both, as Fielding's parody of Richardson turned into *Joseph Andrews*. A lot of science fiction loses much of the impact it could have by saying, 'Well, here we are on Mars, we all know where we are, and we're living in these pressure domes or whatever it is, and life is really very much like it is on earth, except there is a certain climatic difference. . . .' They accept other men's inventions rather than forge their own.

LEWIS: It's only the first journey to a new planet that is of any interest to imaginative people.

AMIS: In your reading of science fiction have you ever come across a writer who's done this properly?

LEWIS: Well, the one you probably disapprove of because he's so very unscientific is David Lindsay, in *Voyage to Arcturus*. It's a remarkable thing, because scientifically it's nonsense, the style is appalling, and yet this ghastly vision comes through.

ALDISS: It didn't come through to me.

AMIS: Nor me. Still . . . Victor Gollancz told me a very interesting remark of Lindsay's about *Arcturus*; he said, 'I shall never appeal to a large public at all, but I think that as long as our civilization lasts one person a year will read me.' I respect that attitude.

LEWIS: Quite so. Modest and becoming. I also agree with something you said in a preface, I believe it was, that some science fiction really does deal with issues far more serious than those realistic fiction deals with; real problems about human destiny and so on. Do you remember that story about the man who meets a female monster landed from another planet with all its cubs hanging round it? It's obviously starving, and he offers them thing after thing to eat; they immediately vomit it up, until one of the young fastens on him, begins sucking his blood, and immediately begins to revive. This female creature is utterly unhuman, horrible in form; there's a long moment when it looks at the man—they're in a lonely place—and then very sadly it packs up its young, and goes back into its spaceship and goes away. Well now, you could not have a more serious theme than that. What is a footling story about some pair of human lovers compared with that?

AMIS: On the debit side, you often have these marvellous large themes tackled by people who haven't got the mental or moral or stylistic equipment to take them on. A reading of more recent science fiction shows that writers are getting more capable of tackling them. Have you read Walter Miller's *Canticle for Leibowitz*? Have you any comments on that?

LEWIS: I thought it was pretty good. I only read it once; mind you, a book's no good to me until I've read it two or three times—I'm going to read it again. It was a major work, certainly.

AMIS: What did you think about its religious feeling?

LEWIS: It came across very well. There were bits of the actual writing which one could quarrel with, but on the whole it was well imagined and well executed.

AMIS: Have you seen James Blish's novel *A Case of Conscience*? Would you agree that to write a religious novel that isn't concerned with details of ecclesiastical practice and the numbing minutiae of history and so on, science fiction would be the natural outlet for this?

LEWIS: If you have a religion it must be cosmic; therefore it seems to me odd that this *genre* was so late in arriving.

ALDISS: It's been around without attracting critical attention for a long time; the magazines themselves have been going since 1926, although in the beginning they appealed mainly to the technical side. As Amis says, people have come along who can write, as well as think up engineering ideas.

LEWIS: We ought to have said earlier that that's quite a different species of science fiction, about which I say nothing at all; those who were really interested in the technical side of it. It's obviously perfectly legitimate if it's well done.

AMIS: The purely technical and the purely imaginative overlap, don't they?

ALDISS: There are certainly the two streams, and they often overlap, for instance in Arthur Clarke's writings. It can be a rich mixture. Then there's the type of story that's not theological, but it makes a moral point. An example is the Sheckley story about Earth being blasted by radioactivity. The survivors of the human race have gone away to another planet for about a thousand years; they come back to reclaim Earth and find it full of all sorts of gaudy armour-plated creatures, vegetation, etc. One of the party says, 'We'll clear this lot out, make it habitable for man again.' But in the end the decision is, 'Well, we made a mess of the place when it was ours, let's get out and leave it to them.' This story was written about '49, when most people hadn't started thinking round the subject at all.

LEWIS: Yes, most of the earlier stories start from the opposite assumption that we, the human race, are in the right, and everything else is ogres. I may have done a little towards altering that, but the new point of view has come very much in. We've lost our confidence, so to speak.

AMIS: It's all terribly self-critical and self-contemplatory nowadays.

LEWIS: This is surely an enormous gain—a human gain, that people should be thinking that way.

AMIS: The prejudice of supposedly educated persons towards this type of fiction is fantastic. If you pick up a science fiction magazine, particularly *Fantasy and Science Fiction*, the range of interests appealed to and I.Q.s employed, is pretty amazing. It's time more people caught on. We've been telling them about it for some while.

LEWIS: Quite true. The world of serious fiction is very narrow.

AMIS: Too narrow if you want to deal with a broad theme. For instance, Philip Wylie in *The Disappearance* wants to deal with the difference between men and women in a general way, in twentieth century society, unencumbered by local and temporary considerations; his point, as I understand it, is that men and women, shorn of their social roles, are really very much the same. Science fiction, which can presuppose a major change in our environment, is the natural medium for discussing a subject of that kind. Look at the job of dissecting human nastiness carried out in Golding's *Lord of the Flies*.

LEWIS: That can't be science fiction.

AMIS: I would dissent from that. It starts off with a characteristic bit of science fiction situation: that World War III has begun, bombs dropped and all that. . . .

LEWIS: Ah, well, you're now taking the German view that any romance about the future is science fiction. I'm not sure that this is a useful classification.

AMIS: 'Science fiction' is such a hopelessly vague label.

LEWIS: And of course a great deal of it isn't *science* fiction.

Really it's only a negative criterion: anything which is not naturalistic, which is not about what we call the real world.

ALDISS: I think we oughtn't to try to define it, because it's a self-defining thing in a way. We know where we are. You're right, though, about *Lord of the Flies*. The atmosphere is a science fiction atmosphere.

LEWIS: It was a very terrestrial island; the best island, almost, in fiction. Its actual sensuous effect on you is terrific.

ALDISS: Indeed. But it's a laboratory case——

AMIS: —isolating certain human characteristics, to see how they would work out——

LEWIS: The only trouble is that Golding writes so well. In one of his other novels, *The Inheritors*, the detail of every sensuous impression, the light on the leaves and so on, was so good that you couldn't find out what was happening. I'd say it was almost too well done. All these little details you only notice in real life if you've got a high temperature. You couldn't see the wood for the leaves.

ALDISS: You had this in *Pincher Martin*; every feeling in the rocks, when he's washed ashore, is done with a hallucinatory vividness.

AMIS: It is, that's exactly the phrase. I think thirty years ago if you wanted to discuss a general theme you would go to the historical novel; now you would go to what I might describe in a prejudiced way as science fiction. In science fiction you can isolate the factors you want to examine. If you wanted to deal with the theme of colonialism, for instance, as Poul Anderson has done, you don't do it by writing a novel about Ghana or Pakistan——

LEWIS: Which involves you in such a mass of detail that you don't want to go into——

AMIS: You set up worlds in space which incorporate the characteristics you need.

LEWIS: Would you describe Abbott's *Flatland* as science fiction? There's so little effort to bring it into any sensuous—

well, you couldn't do it, and it remains an intellectual theorem. Are you looking for an ashtray? Use the carpet.

AMIS: I was looking for the Scotch, actually.

LEWIS: Oh, yes, do, I beg your pardon. . . . But probably the great work in science fiction is still to come. Futile books about the next world came before Dante, Fanny Burney came before Jane Austen, Marlowe came before Shakespeare.

AMIS: We're getting the prolegomena.

LEWIS: If only the modern highbrow critics could be induced to take it seriously . . .

AMIS: Do you think they ever can?

LEWIS: No, the whole present dynasty has got to die and rot before anything can be done at all.

ALDISS: Splendid!

AMIS: What's holding them up, do you think?

LEWIS: Matthew Arnold made the horrible prophecy that literature would increasingly replace religion. It has, and it's taken on all the features of bitter persecution, great intolerance, and traffic in relics. All literature becomes a sacred text. A sacred text is always exposed to the most monstrous exegesis; hence we have the spectacle of some wretched scholar taking a pure *divertissement* written in the seventeenth century and getting the most profound ambiguities and social criticisms out of it, which of course aren't there at all. . . . It's the discovery of the mare's nest by the pursuit of the red herring. (Laughter.) This is going to go on long after my lifetime; you may be able to see the end of it, I shan't.

AMIS: You think this is so integral a part of the Establishment that people can't overcome——

LEWIS: It's an industry, you see. What would all the people be writing *D. Phil.* theses on if this prop were removed?

AMIS: An instance of this mentality the other day: somebody referred to 'Mr Amis's I suspect rather affected enthusiasm for science fiction. . . .'

LEWIS: Isn't that maddening!

AMIS: You can't really like it.

LEWIS: You must be pretending to be a plain man or something. . . . I've met the attitude again and again. You've probably reached the stage too of having theses written on yourself. I received a letter from an American examiner asking, 'Is it true that you meant this and this and this?' A writer of a thesis was attributing to me views which I have explicitly contradicted in the plainest possible English. They'd be much wiser to write about the dead, who can't answer.

ALDISS: In America, I think science fiction is accepted on a more responsible level.

AMIS: I'm not so sure about that, you know, Brian, because when our anthology *Spectrum I* came out in the States we had less friendly and less understanding treatment from reviewers than we did over here.

LEWIS: I'm surprised at that, because in general all American reviewing is more friendly and generous than in England.

AMIS: People were patting themselves on the back in the States for not understanding what we meant.

LEWIS: This extraordinary pride in being exempt from temptations that you have not yet risen to the level of! Eunuchs boasting of their chastity! (Laughter).

AMIS: One of my pet theories is that serious writers as yet unborn or still at school will soon regard science fiction as a natural way of writing.

LEWIS: By the way, has any science fiction writer yet succeeded in inventing a third sex? Apart from the third sex we all know.

AMIS: Clifford Simak invented a set-up where there were seven sexes.

LEWIS: How rare happy marriages must have been then!

ALDISS: Rather worth striving for perhaps.

LEWIS: Obviously when achieved they'd be wonderful. (Laughter.)

ALDISS: I find I would much rather write science fiction than anything else. The dead weight is so much less there than in the field of the ordinary novel. There's a sense in which you're conquering a fresh country.

AMIS: Speaking as a supposedly realistic novelist, I've written little bits of science fiction and this is such a tremendous liberation.

LEWIS: Well, you're a very ill-used man; you wrote a farce and everyone thought it a damning indictment of Redbrick. I've always had great sympathy for you. They will not understand that a joke is a joke. Everything must be serious.

AMIS: 'A fever chart of society.'

LEWIS: One thing in science fiction that weighs against us very heavily is the horrible shadow of the comics.

ALDISS: I don't know about that. Titbits Romantic Library doesn't really weigh against the serious writer.

LEWIS: That's a fair analogy. All the novelettes didn't kill the ordinary legitimate novel of courtship and love.

ALDISS: There might have been a time when science fiction and comics were weighed together and found wanting, but that at least we've got past.

AMIS: I see the comic books that my sons read, and you have there a terribly vulgar reworking of the themes that science fiction goes in for.

LEWIS: Quite harmless, mind you. This chatter about the moral danger of the comics is absolute nonsense. The real objection is against the appalling draughtsmanship. Yet you'll find the same boy who reads them also reads Shakespeare or Spenser. Children are so terribly catholic. That's my experience with my stepchildren.

ALDISS: This is an English habit, to categorize: that if you read Shakespeare you can't read comics, that if you read science fiction you can't be serious.

AMIS: That's the thing that annoys me.

LEWIS: Oughtn't the word 'serious' to have an embargo slapped on it? 'Serious' ought to mean simply the opposite of comic, whereas now it means 'good' or 'Literature' with a capital L.

ALDISS: You can be serious without being earnest.

LEWIS: Leavis demands moral earnestness; I prefer morality.

AMIS: I'm with you every time on that one.

LEWIS: I mean I'd sooner live among people who don't cheat at cards than among people who are earnest about not cheating at cards. (Laughter.)

AMIS: More Scotch?

LEWIS: Not for me, thank you, help yourself. (Liquid noises.)

AMIS: I think all this ought to stay in, you know—all these remarks about drink.

LEWIS: There's no reason why we shouldn't have a drink. Look, you want to borrow Abbott's *Flatland*, don't you? I must go to dinner I'm afraid. (Hands over *Flatland*.) The original manuscript of the *Iliad* could not be more precious. It's only the ungodly who borroweth and payeth not again.

AMIS (reading):   By A. Square.

LEWIS: But of course the word 'square' hadn't the same sense then.

ALDISS: It's like the poem by Francis Thompson that ends 'She gave me tokens three, a look, a word of her winsome mouth, and a sweet wild raspberry'; there again the meaning has changed. It really was a wild raspberry in Thompson's day. (Laughter.)

LEWIS: Or the lovely one about the Bishop of Exeter, who was giving the prizes at a girls' school. They did a performance of *A Midsummer Night's Dream*, and the poor man stood up afterwards and made a speech and said (piping voice): 'I was very interested in your delightful performance, and among other things I was very interested in seeing for the first time in my life a female Bottom.' (Guffaws.)

Part II
STORIES

THE SHODDY LANDS

Being, as I believe, of sound mind and in normal health, I am sitting down at 11 p.m. to record, while the memory of it is still fresh, the curious experience I had this morning.

It happened in my rooms in college, where I am now writing, and began in the most ordinary way with a call on the telephone. 'This is Durward,' the voice said. 'I'm speaking from the porter's lodge. I'm in Oxford for a few hours. Can I come across and see you?' I said yes, of course. Durward is a former pupil and a decent enough fellow; I would be glad to see him again. When he turned up at my door a few moments later I was rather annoyed to find that he had a young woman in tow. I loathe either men or women who speak as if they were coming to see you alone and then spring a husband or a wife, a fiancé or a fiancée on you. One ought to be warned.

The girl was neither very pretty nor very plain, and of course she ruined my conversation. We couldn't talk about any of the things Durward and I had in common because that would have meant leaving her out in the cold. And she and Durward couldn't talk about the things they (presumably) had in common because that would have left me out. He introduced her as Peggy and said they were engaged. After that, the three of us just sat and did social patter about the weather and the news.

I tend to stare when I am bored, and I am afraid I must have stared at that girl, without the least interest, a good deal. At any rate I was certainly doing so at the moment when the strange experience began. Quite suddenly, without any faintness or nausea or anything of that sort, I found myself in a wholly different place. The familiar room vanished; Durward and Peggy vanished. I was alone. And I was standing up.

99

My first idea was that something had gone wrong with my eyes. I was not in darkness, nor even in twilight, but everything seemed curiously blurred. There was a sort of daylight, but when I looked up I didn't see anything that I could very confidently call a sky. It might, just possibly, be the sky of a very feature-less, dull, grey day, but it lacked any suggestion of distance. 'Nondescript' was the word I would have used to describe it. Lower down and closer to me, there were upright shapes, vaguely green in colour, but of a very dingy green. I peered at them for quite a long time before it occurred to me that they might be trees. I went nearer and examined them; and the impression they made on me is not easy to put into words. 'Trees of a sort,' or, 'Well, trees, if you call *that* a tree,' or, 'An attempt at trees,' would come near it. They were the crud-est, shabbiest apology for trees you could imagine. They had no real anatomy, even no real branches; they were more like lamp-posts with great, shapeless blobs of green stuck on top of them. Most children could draw better trees from memory.

It was while I was inspecting them that I first noticed the light: a steady, silvery gleam some distance away in the Shoddy Wood. I turned my steps towards it at once, and then first noticed what I was walking on. It was comfortable stuff, soft and cool and springy to the feet; but when you looked down it was horribly disappointing to the eye. It was, in a very rough way, the colour of grass; the colour grass has on a very dull day when you look at it while thinking pretty hard about something else. But there were no separate blades in it. I stooped down and tried to find them; the closer one looked, the vaguer it seemed to become. It had in fact just the same smudged, unfinished quality as the trees: shoddy.

The full astonishment of my adventure was now beginning to descend on me. With it came fear, but, even more, a sort of disgust. I doubt if it can be fully conveyed to anyone who has not had a similar experience. I felt as if I had suddenly been banished from the real, bright, concrete, and prodigally com-plex world into some sort of second-rate universe that had all been put together on the cheap; by an imitator. But I kept on walking towards the silvery light.

Here and there in the shoddy grass there were patches of what looked, from a distance, like flowers. But each patch, when you came close to it, was as bad as the trees and the grass. You couldn't make out what species they were supposed to be. And they had no real stems or petals; they were mere blobs. As for the colours, I could do better myself with a shilling paintbox.

I should have liked very much to believe that I was dreaming, but somehow I knew I wasn't. My real conviction was that I had died. I wished—with a fervour that no other wish of mine has ever achieved—that I had lived a better life.

A disquieting hypothesis, as you see, was forming in my mind. But next moment it was gloriously blown to bits. Amidst all that shoddiness I came suddenly upon daffodils. Real daffodils, trim and cool and perfect. I bent down and touched them; I straightened my back again and gorged my eyes on their beauty. And not only their beauty but—what mattered to me even more at that moment—their, so to speak, honesty; real, honest, finished daffodils, live things that would bear examination.

But where, then, could I be? 'Let's get on to that light. Perhaps everything will be made clear there. Perhaps it is at the centre of this queer place.'

I reached the light sooner than I expected, but when I reached it I had something else to think about. For now I met the Walking Things. I have to call them that, for 'people' is just what they weren't. They were of human size and they walked on two legs; but they were, for the most part, no more like true men than the Shoddy Trees had been like trees. They were indistinct. Though they were certainly not naked, you couldn't make out what sort of clothes they were wearing, and though there was a pale blob at the top of each, you couldn't say they had faces. At least that was my first impression. Then I began to notice curious exceptions. Every now and then one of them became partially distinct; a face, a hat, or a dress would stand out in full detail. The odd thing was that the distinct clothes were always women's clothes, but the distinct faces were always those of men. Both facts made the crowd—at least, to a man of my type—about as uninteresting as it could possibly be. The male faces were not the sort I cared about; a flashy-looking crew—gigolos, fripoons. But they seemed pleased enough with themselves. Indeed they all wore the same look of fatuous admiration.

I now saw where the light was coming from. I was in a sort of street. At least, behind the crowd of Walking Things on each side, there appeared to be shop-windows, and from these the light came. I thrust my way through the crowd on my left— but my thrusting seemed to yield no physical contacts—and had a look at one of the shops.

Here I had a new surprise. It was a jeweller's, and after the vagueness and general rottenness of most things in that queer place, the sight fairly took my breath away. Everything in that window was perfect; every facet on every diamond distinct, every brooch and tiara finished down to the last perfection of intricate detail. It was good stuff too, as even I could see; there must have been hundreds of thousands of pounds' worth of it. 'Thank Heaven!' I gasped. 'But will it keep on?' Hastily I looked at the next shop. It *was* keeping on. This window contained women's frocks. I'm no judge, so I can't say how good they were. The great thing was that they were real, clear, palpable. The shop beyond this one sold women's shoes. And it was still keeping on. They were real shoes; the toe-pinching and very high-heeled sort which, to my mind, ruins even the prettiest foot, but at any rate real.

I was just thinking to myself that some people would not find this place half as dull as I did, when the queerness of the whole thing came over me afresh. 'Where the Hell,' I began, but immediately changed it to 'Where on earth'—for the other word seemed, in all the circumstances, singularly unfortunate— 'Where on earth have I got to? Trees no good; grass no good; sky no good; flowers no good, except the daffodils; people no good; shops, first class. What can that possibly mean?'

The shops, by the way, were all women's shops, so I soon lost interest in them. I walked the whole length of that street, and then, a little way ahead, I saw sunlight.

Not that it was proper sunlight, of course. There was no break in the dull sky to account for it, no beam slanting down. All that, like so many other things in that world, had not been attended to. There was simply a patch of sunlight on the ground, unexplained, impossible (except that it was there), and therefore not at all cheering; hideous, rather, and disquieting. But I had little time to think about it; for something in the centre of that lighted patch—something I had taken for a small building—suddenly moved, and with a sickening shock I realized that I was looking at a gigantic human shape. It turned round. Its eyes looked straight into mine.

It was not only gigantic, but it was the only complete human shape I had seen since I entered that world. It was female. It was lying on sunlit sand, on a beach apparently, though there was no trace of any sea. It was very nearly naked, but it had a wisp of some brightly coloured stuff round its hips and another round its breasts; like what a modern girl wears on a real beach. The general effect was repulsive, but I saw in a moment or two that this was due to the appalling size. Considered abstractly, the giantess had a good figure; almost a perfect figure, if you like the modern type. The face—but as soon as I had really taken in the face, I shouted out.

'Oh, I say! There you are. Where's Durward? And where's this? What's happened to us?'

But the eyes went on looking straight at me and through me. I was obviously invisible and inaudible to her. But there was no doubt who she was. She was Peggy. That is, she was recognizable; but she was Peggy changed. I don't mean only the size. As regards the figure, it was Peggy improved. I don't think anyone could have denied that. As to the face, opinions might differ. I would hardly have called the change an improvement myself. There was no more—I doubt if there was as much—sense or kindness or honesty in this face than in the original Peggy's. But it was certainly more regular. The teeth in particular, which I had noticed as a weak point in the old Peggy, were perfect, as in a good denture. The lips were fuller. The complexion was so perfect that it suggested a very expensive doll. The expression I can best describe by saying that Peggy now looked exactly like the girl in all the advertisements.

If I had to marry either I should prefer the old, unimproved Peggy. But even in Hell I hoped it wouldn't come to that.

And, as I watched, the background—the absurd little bit of sea-beach—began to change. The giantess stood up. She was on a carpet. Walls and windows and furniture grew up around her. She was in a bedroom. Even I could tell it was a very expensive bedroom though not at all my idea of good taste. There were plenty of flowers, mostly orchids and roses, and these were even better finished than the daffodils had been. One great bouquet (with a card attached to it) was as good as any I have ever seen. A door which stood open behind her gave me a view into a bathroom which I should rather like to own, a bathroom with a sunk bath. In it there was a French maid fussing about with towels and bath salts and things. The maid was not nearly so finished as the roses, or even the towels, but what face she had looked more French than any real Frenchwoman's could.

The gigantic Peggy now removed her beach equipment and stood up naked in front of a full-length mirror. Apparently she enjoyed what she saw there; I can hardly express how much I didn't. Partly the size (it's only fair to remember that) but, still more, something that came as a terrible shock to me, though I suppose modern lovers and husbands must be hardened to it. Her body was (of course) brown, like the bodies in the sun-bathing advertisements. But round her hips, and again round her breasts, where the coverings had been, there were two bands of dead white which looked, by contrast, like leprosy. It made me for the moment almost physically sick. What staggered me was that she could stand and admire it. Had she no idea how it would affect ordinary male eyes? A very disagreeable conviction grew in me that this was a subject of no interest to her; that all her clothes and bath salts and two-piece swimsuits, and indeed the voluptuousness of her every look and gesture, had not, and never had had, the meaning which every man would read, and was intended to read, into them. They were a huge overture to an opera in which she had no interest at all; a coronation procession with no Queen at the centre of it; gestures, gestures about nothing.

And now I became aware that two noises had been going for a long time; the only noises I ever heard in that world. But they were coming from outside, from somewhere beyond that low, grey covering which served the Shoddy Lands instead of a sky. Both the noises were knockings; patient knockings, infinitely remote, as if two outsiders, two excluded people, were knocking on the walls of that world. The one was faint, but hard; and with it came a voice saying, 'Peggy, Peggy, let me in.' Durward's voice, I thought. But how shall I describe the other knocking? It was, in some curious way, soft; 'soft as wool and sharp as death,' soft but unendurably heavy, as if at each blow some enormous hand fell on the outside of the Shoddy Sky and covered it completely. And with that knocking came a voice at whose sound my bones turned to water: 'Child, child, child, let me in before the night comes.'

Before the night comes—instantly common daylight rushed back upon me. I was in my own rooms again and my two visitors were before me. They did not appear to notice that anything unusual had happened to me, though, for the rest of that conversation, they might well have supposed I was drunk. I was so happy. Indeed, in a way I was drunk; drunk with the sheer delight of being back in the real world, free, outside the horrible little prison of that land. There were birds singing close to a window; there was real sunlight falling on a panel. That panel needed repainting; but I could have gone down on my knees and kissed its very shabbiness—the precious real, solid thing it was. I noticed a tiny cut on Durward's cheek where he must have cut himself shaving that morning; and I felt the same about it.

Indeed anything was enough to make me happy; I mean, any Thing, as long as it really was a Thing.

Well, those are the facts; everyone may make what he pleases of them. My own hypothesis is the obvious one which will have occurred to most readers. It may be too obvious; I am quite ready to consider rival theories. My view is that by the operation of some unknown psychological—or pathological—law, I was, for a second or so, let into Peggy's mind; at least to the extent of seeing her world, the world as it exists for her. At the centre of that world is a swollen image of herself, remodelled to be as like the girls in the advertisements as possible. Round this are grouped clear and distinct images of the things she really cares about. Beyond that, the whole earth and sky are a vague blur. The daffodils and roses are especially instructive. Flowers only exist for her if they are the sort that can be cut and put in vases or sent as bouquets; flowers in themselves, flowers as you see them in the woods, are negligible.

As I say, this is probably not the only hypothesis which will fit the facts. But it has been a most disquieting experience. Not only because I am sorry for poor Durward. Suppose this sort of thing were to become common? And how if, some other time, I were not the explorer but the explored?

MINISTERING ANGELS

The Monk, as they called him, settled himself on the camp chair beside his bunk and stared through the window at the harsh sand and black-blue sky of Mars. He did not mean to begin his 'work' for ten minutes yet. Not, of course, the work he had been brought there to do. He was the meteorologist of the party, and his work in that capacity was largely done; he had found out whatever could be found out. There was nothing more, within the limited radius he could investigate, to be observed for at least twenty-five days. And meteorology had not been his real motive. He had chosen three years on Mars as the nearest modern equivalent to a hermitage in the desert. He had come there to meditate: to continue the slow, perpetual rebuilding of that inner structure which, in his view, it was the main purpose of life to rebuild. And now his ten minutes' rest was over. He began with his well-used formula. 'Gentle and patient Master, teach me to need men less and to love thee more.' Then to it. There was no time to waste. There were barely six months of this lifeless, sinless, unsuffering wilderness ahead of him. Three years were short . . . but when the shout came he rose out of his chair with the practised alertness of a sailor.

The Botanist in the next cabin responded to the same shout with a curse. His eye had been at the microscope when it came. It was maddening. Constant interruption. A man might as well try to work in the middle of Piccadilly as in this infernal camp. And his work was already a race against time. Six months more . . . and he had hardly begun. The flora of Mars, these tiny, miraculously hardy organisms, the ingenuity of their contrivances to live under all but impossible conditions—it was a feast for a lifetime. He would ignore the shout. But then came the bell. All hands to the main room.

107

The only person who was doing, so to speak, nothing when the shout came was the Captain. To be more exact, he was (as usual) trying to stop thinking about Clare, and get on with his official journal. Clare kept on interrupting from forty million miles away. It was preposterous. '*Would have needed all hands,*' he wrote . . . hands . . . his own hands . . . his own hands, hands, he felt, with eyes in them, travelling over all the warm-cool, soft-firm, smooth, yielding, resisting aliveness of her. 'Shut up, there's a dear,' he said to the photo on his desk. And so back to the journal, until the fatal words '*had been causing me some anxiety*'. Anxiety—oh God, what might be happening to Clare now? How did he know there was a Clare by this time? Anything could happen. He'd been a fool ever to accept this job. What other newly married man in the world would have done it? But it had seemed so sensible. Three years of horrid separation but then . . . oh, they were made for life. He had been promised the post that, only a few months before, he would not have dared to dream of. He'd never need to go to Space again. And all the by-products; the lectures, the book, probably a title. Plenty of children. He knew she wanted that, and so in a queer way (as he began to find) did he. But damn it, the journal. Begin a new paragraph . . . And then the shout came.

It was one of the two youngsters, technicians both, who had given it. They had been together since dinner. At least Paterson had been standing at the open door of Dickson's cabin, shifting from foot to foot and swinging the door, and Dickson had been sitting on his berth and waiting for Paterson to go away.

'What are you talking about, Paterson?' he said. 'Who ever said anything about a quarrel?'

'That's all very well, Bobby,' said the other, 'but we're not friends like we used to be. You know we're not. Oh, *I'm* not blind. I *did* ask you to call me Clifford. And you're always so stand-offish.'

'Oh, get to Hell out of this!' cried Dickson. 'I'm perfectly ready to be good friends with you and everyone else in an ordinary way, but all this gas—like a pair of school girls—I will not stand. Once and for all——'

'Oh look, look, look,' said Paterson. And it was then that Dickson shouted and the Captain came and rang the bell and within twenty seconds they were all crowded behind the biggest of the windows. A spaceship had just made a beautiful landing about a hundred and fifty yards from camp.

'Oh boy!' exclaimed Dickson. 'They're relieving us before our time.'

'Damn their eyes. Just what they would do,' said the Botanist.

Five figures were descending from the ship. Even in space suits it was clear that one of them was enormously fat; they were in no other way remarkable.

'Man the air lock,' said the Captain.

Drinks from their limited store were going round. The Captain had recognized in the leader of the strangers an old acquaintance, Ferguson. Two were ordinary young men, not unpleasant. But the remaining two?

'I don't understand,' said the Captain, 'who exactly—I mean we're delighted to see you all of course—but what exactly . . .?'

'Where are the rest of your party?' said Ferguson.

'We've had two casualties, I'm afraid,' said the Captain. 'Sackville and Dr Burton. It was a most wretched business. Sackville tried eating the stuff we call Martian cress. It drove him fighting mad in a matter of minutes. He knocked Burton down and by sheer bad luck Burton fell in just the wrong position: across that table there. Broke his neck. We got Sackville tied down on a bunk but he was dead before the evening.'

'Hadna he even the gumption to try it on the guinea pig first?' said Ferguson.

'Yes,' said the Botanist. 'That was the whole trouble. The funny thing is that the guinea pig lived. But its behaviour was remarkable. Sackville wrongly concluded that the stuff was alcoholic. Thought he'd invent a new drink. The nuisance is that once Burton was dead, none of us could do a reliable post-mortem on Sackville. Under analysis this vegetable shows——'

'A-a-a-h,' interrupted one of those who had not yet spoken. 'We must beware of oversimplifications. I doubt if the vegetable substance is the real explanation. There are stresses and strains. You are all, without knowing it, in a highly unstable condition, for reasons which are no mystery to a trained psychologist.'

Some of those present had doubted the sex of this creature. Its hair was very short, its nose very long, its mouth very prim, its chin sharp, and its manner authoritative. The voice revealed it as, scientifically speaking, a woman. But no one had had any doubt about the sex of her nearest neighbour, the fat person.

'Oh, dearie,' she wheezed. 'Not now. I tell you straight I'm that flustered and faint, I'll scream if you go on so. Suppose there ain't such a thing as a port and lemon handy? No? Well, a little drop more gin would settle me. It's me stomach reelly.'

The speaker was infinitely female and perhaps in her seventies. Her hair had been not very successfully dyed to a colour not unlike that of mustard. The powder (scented strongly enough to throw a train off the rails) lay like snow drifts in the complex valleys of her creased, many-chinned face.

'Stop,' roared Ferguson. 'Whatever ye do, dinna give her a drap mair to drink.'

' 'E's no 'art, ye see,' said the old woman with a whimper and an affectionate leer directed at Dickson.

'Excuse me,' said the Captain. 'Who are these—ah—ladies and what is this all about?'

'I have been waiting to explain,' said the Thin Woman, and cleared her throat. 'Anyone who has been following World-Opinion-Trends on the problems arising out of the psychological welfare aspect of interplanetary communication will be conscious of the growing agreement that such a remarkable advance inevitably demands of us far-reaching ideological adjustments. Psychologists are now well aware that a forcible inhibition of powerful biological urges over a protracted period is likely to have unforeseeable results. The pioneers of space

travel are exposed to this danger. It would be unenlightened if
a supposed ethicality were allowed to stand in the way of their
protection. We must therefore nerve ourselves to face the view
that immorality, as it has hitherto been called, must no longer
be regarded as unethical——'

'I don't understand that,' said the Monk.

'She means,' said the Captain, who was a good linguist, 'that
what you call fornication must no longer be regarded as im-
moral.'

'That's right, dearie,' said the Fat Woman to Dickson, 'she
only means a poor boy needs a woman now and then. It's only
natural.'

'What was required, therefore,' continued the Thin Woman,
'was a band of devoted females who would take the first step.
This would expose them, no doubt, to obloquy from many
ignorant persons. They would be sustained by the consciousness that they were performing an indispensable function in the
history of human progress.'

'She means you're to have tarts, duckie,' said the Fat Woman
to Dickson.

'Now you're talking,' said he with enthusiasm. 'Bit late in the
day, but better late than never. But you can't have brought
many girls in that ship. And why didn't you bring them in? Or
are they following?'

'We cannot indeed claim,' continued the Thin Woman, who
had apparently not noticed the interruption, 'that the response
to our appeal was such as we had hoped. The personnel of the
first unit of the Woman's Higher Aphrodiso-Therapeutic
Humane Organisation (abbreviated WHAT-HO) is not perhaps . . . well. Many excellent women, university colleagues of
my own, even senior colleagues, to whom I applied, showed
themselves curiously conventional. But at least a start has been
made. And here,' she concluded brightly, 'we are.'

And there, for forty seconds of appalling silence, they were.
Then Dickson's face, which had already undergone certain
contortions, became very red; he applied his handkerchief and

spluttered like a man trying to stifle a sneeze, rose abruptly, turned his back on the company, and hid his face. He stood slightly stooped and you could see his shoulders shaking.

Paterson jumped up and ran towards him; but the Fat Woman, though with infinite gruntings and upheavals, had risen too.

'Get art of it, Pansy,' she snarled at Paterson. 'Lot o' good your sort ever did.' A moment later her vast arms were round Dickson; all the warm, wobbling maternalism of her engulfed him.

'There, sonny,' she said, 'it's goin' to be O.K. Don't cry, honey. Don't cry. Poor boy, then. Poor boy. I'll give you a good time.'

'I think,' said the Captain, 'the young man is laughing, not crying.'

It was the Monk who at this point mildly suggested a meal.

Some hours later the party had temporarily broken up.

Dickson (despite all his efforts the Fat Woman had contrived to sit next to him; she had more than once mistaken his glass for hers) hardly finished his last mouthful when he said to the newly arrived technicians:

'I'd love to see over your ship, if I could.'

You might expect that two men who had been cooped up in that ship so long, and had only taken off their space suits a few minutes ago, would have been reluctant to re-assume the one and return to the other. That was certainly the Fat Woman's view. 'Nar, nar,' she said. 'Don't you go fidgeting, sonny. They seen enough of that ruddy ship for a bit, same as me. 'Tain't good for you to go rushing about, not on a full stomach, like.' But the two young men were marvellously obliging.

'Certainly. Just what I was going to suggest,' said the first. 'O.K. by me, chum,' said the second. They were all three of them out of the air lock in record time.

Across the sand, up the ladder, helmets off, and then:

'What in the name of thunder have you dumped those two bitches on us for?' said Dickson.

'Don't fancy 'em?' said the Cockney stranger. 'The people at 'ome thought as 'ow you'd be a bit sharp set by now. Ungrateful of you, I call it.'

'Very funny to be sure,' said Dickson. 'But it's no laughing matter for us.'

'It hasn't been for us either, you know,' said the Oxford stranger. 'Cheek by jowl with them for eighty-five days. They palled a bit after the first month.'

'You're telling me,' said the Cockney.

There was a disgusted pause.

'Can anyone tell me,' said Dickson at last, 'who in the world, and why in the world, out of all possible women, selected those two horrors to send to Mars?'

'Can't expect a star London show at the back of beyond,' said the Cockney.

'My dear fellow,' said his colleague, 'isn't the thing perfectly obvious? What kind of woman, without force, is going to come and live in this ghastly place—on rations—and play doxy to half a dozen men she's never seen? The Good Time Girls won't come because they know you can't have a good time on Mars. An ordinary professional prostitute won't come as long as she has the slightest chance of being picked up in the cheapest quarter of Liverpool or Los Angeles. And you've got one who hasn't. The only other who'd come would be a crank who believes all that blah about the new ethicality. And you've got one of that too.'

'Simple, ain't it?' said the Cockney.

'Anyone,' said the other, 'except the Fools at the Top could of course have foreseen it from the word go.'

'The only hope now is the Captain,' said Dickson.

'Look, mate,' said the Cockney, 'if you think there's any question of our taking back returned goods, you've 'ad it. Nothing doin'. Our Captain'll 'ave a mutiny to settle if he tries that. Also 'e won't. 'E's 'ad 'is turn. So've we. It's up to you now.'

'Fair's fair, you know,' said the other. 'We've stood all we can.'

'Well,' said Dickson. 'We must leave the two chiefs to fight it out. But discipline or not, there are some things a man can't stand. That bloody schoolmarm——'

'She's a lecturer at a Redbrick university, actually.'

'Well,' said Dickson after a long pause, 'you were going to show me over the ship. It might take my mind off it a bit.'

The Fat Woman was talking to the Monk. '. . . and oh, Father dear, I know you'll think that's the worst of all. I didn't give it up when I could. After me brother's wife died . . . 'e'd 'av 'ad me 'ome with 'im, and money wasn't that short. But I went on, Gawd 'elp me, I went on.'

'Why did you do that, daughter?' said the Monk. 'Did you *like* it?'

'Well not all that, Father. I was never partikler. But you see—oh, Father, I was the goods in those days, though you wouldn't think it now . . . and the poor gentlemen, they did so enjoy it.'

'Daughter,' he said, 'you are not far from the Kingdom. But you were wrong. The desire to give is blessed. But you can't turn bad bank notes into good ones just by giving them away.'

The Captain had also left the table pretty quickly, asking Ferguson to accompany him to his cabin. The Botanist had leaped after them.

'One moment, sir, one moment,' he said excitedly. 'I am a scientist. I'm working at very high pressure already. I hope there is no complaint to be made about my discharge of all those other duties which so incessantly interrupt my work. But if I am going to be expected to waste any more time entertaining those abominable females——'

'When I give you any orders which can be considered *ultra vires*,' said the Captain, 'it will be time to make your protest.'

Paterson stayed with the Thin Woman. The only part of any woman that interested him was her ears. He liked telling

women about his troubles; especially about the unfairness and
unkindness of other men. Unfortunately the lady's idea was
that the interview should be devoted either to Aphrodisio-
Therapy or to instruction in psychology. She saw, indeed, no
reason why the two operations should not be carried out simul-
taneously; it is only untrained minds that cannot hold more
than one idea. The difference between these two conceptions of
the conversation was well on its way to impairing its success.
Paterson was becoming ill-tempered; the lady remained bright
and patient as an iceberg.

'But as I was saying,' grumbled Paterson, 'what I do think
so rotten is a fellow being quite fairly decent one day and
then——'

'Which just illustrates my point. These tensions and malad-
justments are bound, under the unnatural conditions, to arise.
And provided we disinfect the obvious remedy of all those
sentimental or—which is quite as bad—prurient associations
which the Victorian Age attached to it——'

'But I haven't yet told you. Listen. Only two days ago——'

'One moment. This ought to be regarded like any other in-
jection. If once we can persuade——'

'How any fellow can take a pleasure——'

'I agree. The association of it with pleasure (that is purely
an adolescent fixation) may have done incalculable harm.
Rationally viewed——'

'I say, you're getting off the point.'

'One moment——'

The dialogue continued.

They had finished looking over the spaceship. It was certainly a beauty. No one afterwards remembered who had first
said, 'Anyone could manage a ship like this.'

Ferguson sat quietly smoking while the Captain read the
letter he had brought him. He didn't even look in the Captain's
direction. When at last conversation began there was so much
circumambient happiness in the cabin that they took a long

time to get down to the difficult part of their business. The Captain seemed at first wholly occupied with its comic side.

'Still,' he said at last, 'it has its serious side too. The impertinence of it, for one thing! Do they think——'

'Ye maun recall,' said Ferguson, 'they're dealing with an absolutely new situation.'

'Oh, *new* be damned! How does it differ from men on whalers, or even on windjammers in the old days? Or on the North West Frontier? It's about as new as people being hungry when food was short.'

'Eh mon, but ye're forgettin' the new light of modern psychology.'

'I think those two ghastly women have already learned some newer psychology since they arrived. Do they really suppose every man in the world is so combustible that he'll jump into the arms of any woman whatever?'

'Aye, they do. They'll be sayin' you and your party are verra abnormal. I wadna put it past them to be sending you out wee packets of hormones next.'

'Well, if it comes to that, do they suppose men would volunteer for a job like this unless they could, or thought they could, or wanted to try if they could, do without women?'

'Then there's the new ethics, forbye.'

'Oh stow it, you old rascal. What is new there either? Who ever tried to live clean except a minority who had a religion or were in love? They'll try it still on Mars, as they did on Earth. As for the majority, did they ever hesitate to take their pleasures wherever they could get them? The ladies of the profession know better. Did you ever see a port or a garrison town without plenty of brothels? Who are the idiots on the Advisory Council who started all this nonsense?'

'Och, a pack o' daft auld women (in trousers for the maist part) who like onything sexy, and onything scientific, and onything that makes them feel important. And this gives them all three pleasures at once, ye ken.'

'Well, there's only one thing for it, Ferguson. I'm not going to have either your Mistress Overdone or your Extension lecturer here. You can just——'

'Now there's no manner of use talkin' that way. I did my job. Another voyage with sic a cargo o' livestock I will not face. And my two lads the same. There'd be mutiny and murder.'

'But you must, I'm——'

At that moment a blinding flash came from without and the earth shook.

'Ma ship! Ma ship!' cried Ferguson. Both men peered out on empty sand. The spaceship had obviously made an excellent take-off.

'But what's happened?' said the Captain. 'They haven't——'

'Mutiny, desertion, and theft of a government ship, that's what's happened,' said Ferguson. 'Ma twa lads and your Dickson are awa' hame.'

'But good Lord, they'll get Hell for this. They've ruined their careers. They'll be——'

'Aye. Nae dout. And they think it cheap at the price. Ye'll be seeing why, maybe, before ye are a fortnight older.'

A gleam of hope came into the Captain's eyes. 'They couldn't have taken the women with them?'

'Talk sense, mon, talk sense. Or if ye hanna ony sense, use your ears.'

In the buzz of excited conversation which became every moment more audible from the main room, female voices could be intolerably distinguished.

As he composed himself for his evening meditation the Monk thought that perhaps he had been concentrating too much on 'needing less' and that must be why he was going to have a course (advanced) in 'loving more'. Then his face twitched into a smile that was not all mirth. He was thinking of the Fat Woman. Four things made an exquisite chord. First the horror of all she had done and suffered. Secondly, the pity—thirdly, the comicality—of her belief that she could still excite desire; fourthly, her bless'd ignorance of that utterly different loveliness which already existed within her and which, under grace, and with such poor direction as even he could supply, might one day set her, bright in the land of brightness, beside the Magdalene.

But wait! There was yet a fifth note in the chord. 'Oh, Master,' he murmured, 'forgive—or can you enjoy?—my absurdity also. I had been supposing you sent me on a voyage of forty million miles merely for my own spiritual convenience.'

FORMS OF THINGS UNKNOWN

['. . . *that what was myth in one world might always be fact in some other.'* PERELANDRA]

'Before the class breaks up, gentlemen,' said the instructor, 'I should like to make some reference to a fact which is known to some of you, but probably not yet to all. High Command, I need not remind you, has asked for a volunteer for yet one more attempt on the Moon. It will be the fourth. You know the history of the previous three. In each case the explorers landed unhurt; or at any rate alive. We got their messages. Every message short, some apparently interrupted. And after that never a word, gentlemen. I think the man who offers to make the fourth voyage has about as much courage as anyone I've heard of. And I can't tell you how proud it makes me that he is one of my own pupils. He is in this room at this moment. We wish him every possible good fortune. Gentlemen, I ask you to give three cheers for Lieutenant John Jenkin.'

Then the class became a cheering crowd for two minutes; after that a hurrying, talkative crowd in the corridor. The two biggest cowards exchanged the various family reasons which had deterred them from volunteering themselves. The knowing man said, 'There's something behind all this.' The vermin said, 'He always was a chap who'd do anything to get himself into the limelight.' But most just shouted out 'Jolly good show, Jenkin,' and wished him luck.

Ward and Jenkin got away together into a pub.

'You kept this pretty dark,' said Ward. 'What's yours?'

'A pint of draught Bass,' said Jenkin.

'Do you want to talk about it?' said Ward rather awkwardly

when the drinks had come. 'I mean—if you won't think I'm butting in—it's not just because of that girl, is it?'

That girl was a young woman who was thought to have treated Jenkin rather badly.

'Well,' said Jenkin. 'I don't suppose I'd be going if she had married me. But it's not a spectacular attempt at suicide or any rot of that sort. I'm not depressed. I don't feel anything particular about her. Not much interested in women at all, to tell you the truth. Not now. A bit petrified.'

'What is it then?'

'Sheer unbearable curiosity. I've read those three little messages over and over till I know them by heart. I've heard every theory there is about what interrupted them. I've——'

'Is it certain they were all interrupted? I thought one of them was supposed to be complete.'

'You mean Traill and Henderson? I think it was as incomplete as the others. First there was Stafford. He went alone, like me.'

'Must you? I'll come, if you'll have me.'

Jenkin shook his head. 'I knew you would,' he said. 'But you'll see in a moment why I don't want you to. But to go back to the messages. Stafford's was obviously cut short by something. It went: *Stafford from within 50 miles of Point XO308 on the Moon. My landing was excellent. I have*—then silence. Then come Traill and Henderson. *We have landed. We are perfectly well. The ridge M392 is straight ahead of me as I speak. Over.*'

'What do you make of *Over*?'

'Not what you do. You think it means *finis*—the message is over. But who in the world, speaking to Earth from the Moon for the first time in all history, would have so little to say—if he *could* say any more? As if he'd crossed to Calais and sent his grandmother a card to say "Arrived safely". The thing's ludicrous.'

'Well, what do *you* make of *Over*?'

'Wait a moment. The last lot were Trevor, Woodford, and Fox. It was Fox who sent the message. Remember it?'

'Probably not so accurately as you.'

'Well, it was this. *This is Fox speaking. All has gone wonderfully well. A perfect landing. You shot pretty well for I'm on Point XO308 at this moment. Ridge M392 straight ahead. On my left, far away across the crater I see the big peaks. On my right I see the Yerkes cleft. Behind me.* Got it?'

'I don't see the point.'

'Well Fox was cut off the moment he said *behind me*. Supposing Traill was cut off in the middle of saying "Over my shoulder I can see" or "Over behind me" or something like that?'

'You mean?——'

'All the evidence is consistent with the view that everything went well till the speaker looked behind him. Then something got him.'

'What sort of a something?'

'That's what I want to find out. One idea in my head is this. Might there be something on the Moon—or something psychological about the experience of landing on the Moon—which drives men fighting mad?'

'I see. You mean Fox looked round just in time to see Trevor and Woodford preparing to knock him on the head?'

'Exactly. And Traill—for it was Traill—just in time to see Henderson a split second before Henderson murdered him. And that's why I'm not going to risk having a companion; least of all my best friend.'

'This doesn't explain Stafford.'

'No. That's why one can't rule out the other hypothesis.'

'What's it?'

'Oh, that whatever killed them all was something they found there. Something lunar.'

'You're surely not going to suggest life on the Moon at this time of day?'

'The word *life* always begs the question. Because, of course, it suggests organization as we know it on Earth—with all the chemistry which organization involves. Of course there could hardly be anything of that sort. But there might—I at any rate can't say there couldn't—be masses of matter capable of movements determined from within, determined, in fact, by intentions.'

'Oh Lord, Jenkin, that's nonsense. Animated stones, no doubt! That's mere science fiction or mythology.'

'Going to the Moon at all was once science fiction. And as for mythology, haven't they found the Cretan labyrinth?'

'And all it really comes down to,' said Ward, 'is that no one has ever come back from the Moon, and no one, so far as we know, ever survived there for more than a few minutes. Damn the whole thing.' He stared gloomily into his tankard.

'Well,' said Jenkin cheerily, 'somebody's got to go. The whole human race isn't going to be licked by any blasted satellite.'

'I might have known that was your real reason,' said Ward.

'Have another pint and don't look so glum,' said Jenkin. 'Anyway, there's loads of time. I don't suppose they'll get me off for another six months at the earliest.'

But there was hardly any time. Like any man in the modern world on whom tragedy has descended or who has undertaken a high enterprise, he lived for the next few months a life not unlike that of a hunted animal. The Press, with all their cameras and notebooks were after him. They did not care in the least whether he was allowed to eat or sleep or whether they made a nervous wreck of him before he took off. 'Flesh-flies,' he called them. When forced to address them, he always said, 'I wish I could take you all with me.' But he reflected also that a Saturn's ring of dead (and burnt) reporters circling round his space-ship might get on his nerves. They would hardly make 'the silence of those eternal spaces' any more homelike.

The take-off when it came was a relief. But the voyage was worse than he had ever anticipated. Not physically—on that side it was nothing worse than uncomfortable—but in the emotional experience. He had dreamed all his life, with mingled terror and longing, of those eternal spaces; of being utterly 'outside', in the sky. He had wondered if the agoraphobia of that roofless and bottomless vacuity would overthrow his

reason. But the moment he had been shut into his ship there
descended upon him the suffocating knowledge that the real
danger of space-travel is claustrophobia. You have been put in
a little metal container; somewhat like a cupboard, very like a
coffin. You can't see out; you can see things only on the screen.
Space and the stars are just as remote as they were on the earth.
Where you are is always your world. The sky is never where you
are. All you have done is to exchange a large world of earth and
rock and water and clouds for a tiny world of metal.

This frustration of a life-long desire bit deeply into his mind
as the cramped hours passed. It was not, apparently, so easy
to jump out of one's destiny. Then he became conscious of
another motive which, unnoticed, had been at work on him
when he volunteered. That affair with the girl had indeed frozen
him stiff; petrified him, you might say. He wanted to feel again,
to be flesh, not stone. To feel anything, even terror. Well, on
this trip there would be terrors enough before all was done.
He'd be wakened, never fear. That part of his destiny at least
he felt he could shake off.

The landing was not without terror, but there were so many
gimmicks to look after, so much skill to be exercised, that it
did not amount to very much. But his heart was beating a little
more noticeably than usual as he put the finishing touches to
his space-suit and climbed out. He was carrying the transmission apparatus with him. It felt, as he had expected, as light
as a loaf. But he was not going to send any message in a hurry.
That might be where all the others had gone wrong. Anyway,
the longer he waited the longer those press-men would be kept
out of their beds waiting for their story. Do 'em good.

The first thing that struck him was that his helmet had been
too lightly tinted. It was painful to look at all in the direction
of the sun. Even the rock—it was, after all, rock not dust
(which disposed of one hypothesis)—was dazzling. He put down
the apparatus; tried to take in the scene.

The surprising thing was how small it looked. He thought he
could account for this. The lack of atmosphere forbade nearly

all the effect that distance has on earth. The serrated boundary of the crater was, he knew, about twenty-five miles away. It looked as if you could have touched it. The peaks looked as if they were a few feet high. The black sky, with its inconceivable multitude and ferocity of stars, was like a cap forced down upon the crater; the stars only just out of his reach. The impression of a stage-set in a toy theatre, therefore of something arranged, therefore of something waiting for him, was at once disappointing and oppressive. Whatever terrors there might be, here too agoraphobia would not be one of them.

He took his bearings and the result was easy enough. He was, like Fox and his friends, almost exactly on Point XO308. But there was no trace of human remains.

If he could find any, he might have some clue as to how they died. He began to hunt. He went in each circle further from the ship. There was no danger of losing it in a place like this.

Then he got his first real shock of fear. Worse still, he could not tell what was frightening him. He only knew that he was engulfed in sickening unreality; seemed neither to be where he was nor to be doing what he did. It was also somehow connected with an experience long ago. It was something that had happened in a cave. Yes; he remembered now. He had been walking along supposing himself alone and then noticed that there was always a sound of other feet following him. Then in a flash he realised what was wrong. This was the exact reverse of the experience in the cave. Then there had been too many footfalls. Now there were too few. He walked on hard rock as silently as a ghost. He swore at himself for a fool—as if every child didn't know that a world without air would be a world without noise. But the silence, though explained, became none the less terrifying.

He had now been alone on the Moon for perhaps thirty-five minutes. It was then that he noticed the three strange things.

The sun's rays were roughly at right angles to his line of sight, so that each of the things had a bright side and a dark side; for each dark side a shadow like Indian ink lay out on the rock. He thought they looked like Belisha beacons. Then he thought they looked like huge apes. They were about the height of a man. They were indeed like clumsily shaped men. Except—he resisted an impulse to vomit—that they had no heads.

They had something instead. They were (roughly) human up to their shoulders. Then, where the head should have been, there was utter monstrosity—a huge spherical block; opaque, featureless. And every one of them looked as if it had that moment stopped moving or were at that moment about to move.

Ward's phrase about 'animated stones' darted up hideously from his memory. And hadn't he himself talked of something that we couldn't call life, not in our sense, something that could nevertheless produce locomotion and have intentions? Something which, at any rate, shared with life life's tendency to kill? If there were such creatures—mineral equivalents to organisms —they could probably stand perfectly still for a hundred years without feeling any strain.

Were they aware of him? What had they for senses? The opaque globes on their shoulders gave no hint.

There comes a moment in nightmare, or sometimes in real battle, when fear and courage both dictate the same course: to rush, planless, upon the thing you are afraid of. Jenkin sprang upon the nearest of the three abominations and rapped his gloved knuckles against its globular top.

Ach!—he'd forgotten. No noise. All the bombs in the world might burst here and make no noise. Ears are useless on the Moon.

He recoiled a step and next moment found himself sprawling on the ground. 'This is how they all died,' he thought.

But he was wrong. The figure above him had not stirred. He was quite undamaged. He got up again and saw what he had tripped over.

It was a purely terrestrial object. It was, in fact, a transmission set. Not exactly like his own, but an earlier and supposedly inferior model—the sort Fox would have had.

As the truth dawned on him an excitement very different

from that of terror seized him. He looked at their mis-shaped bodies; then down at his own limbs. Of course; that was what one looked like in a space suit. On his own head there was a similar monstrous globe, but fortunately not an opaque one. He was looking at three statues of spacemen: at statues of Trevor, Woodford, and Fox.

But then the Moon must have inhabitants; and rational inhabitants; more than that, artists.

And what artists! You might quarrel with their taste, for no line anywhere in any of the three statues had any beauty. You could not say a word against their skill. Except for the head and face inside each headpiece, which obviously could not be attempted in such a medium, they were perfect. Photographic accuracy had never reached such a point on earth. And though they were faceless you could see from the set of their shoulders and indeed of their whole bodies, that a momentary pose had been exactly seized. Each was the statue of a man turning to look behind him. Months of work had doubtless gone to the carving of each; it caught that instantaneous gesture like a stone snapshot.

Jenkin's idea was now to send his message at once. Before anything happened to himself, Earth must hear this amazing news. He set off in great strides, and presently in leaps—now first enjoying lunar gravitation—for his ship and his own set. He was happy now. He *had* escaped his destiny. Petrified, eh? No more feelings? Feelings enough to last him forever.

He fixed the set so that he could stand with his back to the sun. He worked the gimmicks. 'Jenkin, speaking from the Moon,' he began.

His own huge black shadow lay out before him. There is no noise on the Moon. Up from behind the shoulders of his own shadow another shadow pushed its way along the dazzling rock. It was that of a human head. And what a head of hair. It was all rising, writhing—swaying in the wind perhaps. Very thick the hairs looked. Then, as he turned in terror, there flashed through his mind the thought, 'But there's no wind. No air. It can't be *blowing* about.' His eyes met hers.

AFTER TEN YEARS

For several minutes now Yellowhead had thought seriously of moving his right leg. Though the discomfort of his present position was almost unbearable, the move was not lightly to be undertaken. Not in this darkness, packed so close as they were. The man next to him (he could not remember who it was) might be asleep or might at least be tolerably comfortable, so that he would growl or even curse if you pressed or pushed him. A quarrel would be fatal; and some of the company were hot-tempered and loud-voiced enough. There were other things to avoid too. The place stank vilely; they had been shut up for hours with all their natural necessities (fears included) upon them. Some of them—skeery young fools—had vomited. But that had been when the whole thing moved, so there was some excuse; they had been rolled to and fro in their prison, left, right, up and (endlessly, sickeningly) down; worse than a storm at sea.

That had been hours ago. He wondered how many hours. It must be evening by now. The light which, at first, had come down to them through the sloping shaft at one end of the accursed contraption, had long ago disappeared. They were in perfect blackness. The humming of insects had stopped. The stale air was beginning to be chilly. It must be well after sunset.

Cautiously he tried to extend his leg. It met at once hard muscle; defiantly hard muscle in the leg of someone who was wide awake and wouldn't budge. So that line was no good. Yellowhead drew back his foot further and brought his knee up under his chin. It was not a position you could hold for long, but for a moment it was relief. Oh, if once they were out of this thing . . .

And when they were, what next? Plenty of chance to get the

fidgets out of one's limbs then. There might be two hours of
pretty hard work; not more, he thought. That is, if everything
went well? And after that? After that, he would find the Wicked
Woman. He was sure he would find her. It was known that she
had been still alive within the last month. He'd get her all right.
And he would do such things to her. . . . Perhaps he would torture her. He told himself, but all in words, about the tortures.
He had to do it in words because no pictures of it would come
into his mind. Perhaps he'd have her first; brutally, insolently,
like an enemy and a conqueror; show her she was no more than
any other captured girl. And she was no more than any girl.
The pretence that she was somehow different, the endless
flattery, was most likely what had sent her wrong to begin with.
People were such fools.

Perhaps, when he had had her himself, he'd give her to the
other prisoners to make sport for them. Excellent. But he'd pay
the slaves out for touching her too. The picture of what he'd
do to the slaves formed itself quite easily.

He had to extend his leg again, but now he found that the
place where it had lain had somehow filled itself up. That other
man had overflowed into it and Yellowhead was the worse off
for his move. He twisted himself round a little so as to rest
partly on his left hip. This too was something he had to thank
the Wicked Woman for; it was on her account that they were
all smothering in this den.

But he wouldn't torture her. He saw that was nonsense. Torture was all very well for getting information; it was no real use
for revenge. All people under torture have the same face and
make the same noise. You lose the person you hated. And it
never makes them feel wicked. And she was young; only a girl.
He could pity her. There were tears in his eyes. Perhaps it
would be better just to kill her. No rape, no punishments; just a
solemn, stately, mournful, almost regretful killing, like a sacrifice.

But they had to get out first. The signal from outside ought
to have come hours ago. Perhaps all the others, all round him
in the dark, were quite certain that something had gone wrong,

128

and each was waiting for someone else to say it. There was no difficulty in thinking of things that might have gone wrong. He saw now that the whole plan had been crazy from the beginning. What was there to prevent their all being roasted alive where they sat? Why should their own friends from outside ever find them? Or find them alone and unguarded? How if no signal ever came and they never got out at all? They were in a death-trap.

He dug his nails into his palms and shut off these thoughts by mere force. For everyone knew, and everyone had said before they got in, that these were the very thoughts that would come during the long wait, and that at all costs you must not think them; whatever else you pleased, but not those.

He started thinking about the Woman again. He let pictures rise in the dark, all kinds; clothed, naked, asleep, awake, drinking, dancing, nursing the child, laughing. A little spark of desire began to glow; the old, ever-renewed astonishment. He blew on it most deliberately. Nothing like lust for keeping fear at a distance and making time pass.

But nothing would make the time pass.

Hours later cramp woke him with a scream on his mouth. Instantly a hand was thrust beneath his chin forcing his teeth shut. 'Quiet. Listen,' said several voices. For now at last there was a noise from outside; a tapping from beneath the floor. Oh Zeus, Zeus make it to be real; don't let it be a dream. There it came again, five taps and then five and then two, just as they had arranged. The darkness around him was full of elbows and knuckles. Everyone seemed to be moving. 'Get back there,' said someone. 'Give us room.' With a great wrenching sound the trap door came up. A square of lesser darkness—almost, by comparison, of light—appeared at Yellowhead's feet. The joy of mere seeing, of seeing anything at all, and the deep draughts he took of the clean, cold air, put everything else out of his mind for the moment. Someone beside him was paying a rope out through the opening.

'Get on then,' said a voice in his ear.

He tried to, then gave it up. 'I must unstiffen first,' he said.

'Then out of my way,' said the voice. A burly figure thrust itself forward and went hand over hand down the rope and out of sight. Another and another followed. Yellowhead was almost the last.

And so, breathing deep and stretching their limbs, they all stood by the feet of the great wooden horse with the stars above them, and shivered a little in the cold night wind that blew up the narrow streets of Troy.

II

'Steady, men,' said Yellowhead Menelaus. 'Don't go inside yet. Get your breath.' Then in a lower voice, 'Get in the doorway, Eteoneus, and don't let them in. We don't want them to start looting yet.'

It was less than two hours since they had left the horse, and all had gone extremely well. They had had no difficulty in finding the Scaean gate. Once you are inside a city's wall every unarmed enemy is either a guide or a dead man, and most choose to be the first. There was a guard at the gate, of course, but they had disposed of it quickly and, what was best of all, with very little noise. In twenty minutes they had got the gate open and the main army was pouring in. There had been no serious fighting till they reached the citadel. It had been lively enough there for a bit, but Yellowhead and his Spartans had suffered little, because Agamemnon had insisted on leading the van. Yellowhead had thought, all things considered, that this place should have been his own, for the whole war was in a sense his war, even if Agamemnon were the King of Kings and his elder brother. Once they were inside the outer circling wall of the citadel, the main body had set about the inner gate which was very strong, while Yellowhead and his party had been sent round to find a back way in. They had overpowered what defence they found there and now they stopped to pant and mop their faces and clean their swords and spear-blades.

After Ten Years

This little porch opened on a stone platform circled by a wall that was only breast-high. Yellowhead leaned his elbow on it and looked down. He could not see the stars now. Troy was burning. The glorious fires, the loud manes and beards of flame and the billows of smoke, blotted out the sky. Beyond the city the whole countryside was lit up with the glare; you could see even the familiar and hated beach itself and the endless line of ships. Thank the gods, they would soon bid good-bye to that!

While they had been fighting he had never given Helen a thought and had been happy; he had felt himself once more a king and a soldier, and every decision he made had proved right. As the sweat dried, though he was thirsty as an oven and had a smarting little gash above his knee, some of the sweetness of victory began to come into his mind. Agamemnon no doubt would be called the City-Sacker. But Yellowhead had a notion that when the story reached the minstrels he himself would be the centre of it. The pith of the song would be how Menelaus King of Sparta had won back from the barbarians the most beautiful woman in the world. He did not yet know whether he would take her back to his bed or not, but he would certainly not kill her. Destroy a trophy like that?

A shiver reminded him that the men would be getting cold and that some might be losing their nerve. He thrust through the mass and went up the shallow steps to where Eteoneus was standing. 'I'll come here,' he said. 'You bring up the rear and chivvy them on.' Then he raised his voice. 'Now, friends,' he said, 'we're going in. Keep together and keep your eyes open. There may be mopping up to do. And they're probably holding some passage further in.'

He led them for a few paces under darkness past fat pillars and then out into a small court open to the sky; brilliantly lit at one moment as the flames shot up from some house collapsing in the outer city and then again almost totally dark. It was clearly slaves' quarters. A chained dog, standing on its hind legs, barked at them with passionate hatred from one corner and there were piles of garbage. And then—'Ah! Would you?' he

131

cried. Armed men were pouring out of a doorway straight
ahead. They were princes of the blood by the look of their
armour, one of them little more than a child, and they had the
look—Yellowhead had seen it before in conquered towns—of
men who are fighting to die rather than to kill. They are the
most dangerous sort while they last. He lost three men there,
but they got all the Trojans. Yellowhead bent down and
finished off the boy who was still writhing like a damaged insect.
Agamemnon had often told him that this was a waste of time,
but he hated to see them wriggle.

The next court was different. There seemed to be much
carved work on the walls, the pavement was of blue and white
flagstones, and there was a pool in the middle. Female shapes,
hard to see accurately in the dancing firelight, scattered away
from them to left and right into the shadows, like rats when you
come suddenly into a cellar. The old ones wailed in high, sense-
less voices as they hobbled. The girls screamed. His men were
after them; as if terriers had been sent in among the rats. Here
and there a scream ended in a titter.

'None of that,' shouted Yellowhead. 'You can have all the
women you want tomorrow. Not now.'

A man close beside him had actually dropped his spear to
have both hands free for the exploration of a little, dark sixteen-
year-old who looked like an Egyptian. His fat lips were feeding
on her face. Yellowhead fetched him one across the buttocks
with the flat of his sword.

'Let her go, with a curse on you,' he said, 'or I'll cut your
throat.'

'Get on. Get on,' shouted Eteoneus from behind. 'Follow the
King.'

Through an archway a new and steadier light appeared; lamp-
light. They came into a roofed place. It was extraordinarily
still and they themselves became still as they entered it. The
noise of the assault and the battering ram at the main gate on
the other side of the castle seemed to be coming from a great
distance. The lamp flames were unshaken. The room was full of

a sweet smell, you could smell the costliness of it. The floor was
covered with soft stuff, dyed in crimson. There were cushions
of silk piled upon couches of ivory; panels of ivory also on the
walls and squares of jade brought from the end of the world.
The room was of cedar and gilded beams. They were humiliated
by the richness. There was nothing like this at Mycenae, let
alone at Sparta; hardly perhaps at Cnossus. And each man
thought, 'And thus the barbarians have lived these ten years,
while we sweated and shivered in huts on the beach.'

'It was time it ended,' said Yellowhead to himself. He saw a
great vase so perfect in shape that you would think it had grown
like a flower, made of some translucent stuff he had never seen
before. It stupefied him for a second. Then, in retaliation, he
drove at it as hard as he could with the butt-end of his spear
and shattered it into a hundred tinkling and shining fragments.
His men laughed. They began following his example—breaking,
tearing. But it disgusted him when they did it.

'Try what's behind the doors,' he said. There were many
doors. From behind some of them they dragged or led the
women out; not slaves but kings' wives or daughters. The men
attempted no foolery; they knew well enough these were re-
served for their betters. And their faces showed ghastly. There
was a curtained doorway ahead. He swept the heavy, intri-
cately embroidered, stuff aside and went in. Here was an inner,
smaller, more exquisite room.

It was many-sided. Four very slender pillars held up the
painted roof and between them hung a lamp that was a marvel of
goldsmith's work. Beneath it, seated with her back against one
of the pillars, a woman, no longer young, sat with her distaff,
spinning; as a great lady might sit in her own house a thousand
miles away from the war.

Yellowhead had been in ambushes. He knew what it costs
even a trained man to be still on the brink of deadly danger. He
thought, 'That woman must have the blood of gods in her.' He
resolved he would ask her where Helen was to be found. He
would ask her courteously.

She looked up and stopped her spinning but still she did not move.

'The child,' she said in a low voice. 'Is she still alive? Is she well?' Then, helped by the voice, he recognized her. And with the first second of his recognition all that had made the very shape of his mind for eleven years came tumbling down in irretrievable ruin. Neither that jealousy nor that lust, that rage nor that tenderness, could ever be revived. There was nothing inside him appropriate to what he saw. For a moment there was nothing inside him at all.

For he had never dreamed she would be like this; never dreamed that the flesh would have gathered under her chin, that the face could be so plump and yet so drawn, that there would be grey hair at her temples and wrinkles at the corners of her eyes. Even her height was less than he remembered. The smooth glory of her skin which once made her seem to cast a light from her arms and shoulders was all gone. An ageing woman; a sad, patient, composed woman, asking for her daughter; for their daughter.

The astonishment of it jerked a reply out of him before he well knew what he was doing. 'I've not seen Hermione for ten years,' he said. Then he checked himself. How had she the effrontery to ask like that, just as an honest wife might? It would be monstrous for them to fall into an ordinary husbandly and wifely conversation as if nothing had come between. And yet what had come between was less disabling than what he now encountered.

About that he suffered a deadlock of conflicting emotions. It served her right. Where was her vaunted beauty now? Vengeance? Her mirror punished her worse than he could every day. But there was pity too. The story that she was the daughter of Zeus, the fame that had made her a legend on both sides of the Aegean, all dwindled to this, all destroyed like the vase he had shivered five minutes ago. But there was shame too. He had dreamed of living in stories as the man who won back the most beautiful woman in the world, had he? And what he had won back was this. For this Patroclus and Achilles had died. If he appeared before the army leading this as his prize, as their prize, what could follow but universal curses or universal laughter? Inextinguishable laughter to the world's end. Then it darted into his mind that the Trojans must have known it for years. They too must have roared with laughter every time a Greek fell. Not only the Trojans, the gods too. They had known all along. It had diverted them through him to stir up Agamemnon and through Agamemnon to stir up all Greece, and set two nations by the ears for ten winters, all for a woman whom no one would buy in any market except as a housekeeper or a nurse. The bitter wind of divine derision blew in his face. All for nothing, all a folly and himself the prime fool.

He could hear his own men clattering into the room behind him. Something would have to be decided. Helen did and said nothing. If she had fallen at his feet and begged for forgiveness; if she had risen up and cursed him; if she had stabbed herself. . . . But she only waited with her hands (they were knuckley hands now) on her lap. The room was filling with men. It would be terrible if they recognized Helen; perhaps worse if he had to tell them. The oldest of the soldiers was staring at her very hard and looking from her to Yellowhead.

'So!' said the man at last, almost with a chuckle. 'Well, by all the——'

Eteoneus nudged him into silence. 'What do you wish us to do, Menelaus?' he asked, looking at the floor.

'With the prisoners—the other prisoners?' said Yellowhead. 'You must detail a guard and get them all down to camp. The rest at Nestor's place, for the distribution. The Queen—this one—to our own tents.'

'Bound?' said Eteoneus in his ear.

'It's not necessary,' said Yellowhead. It was a loathsome question: either answer was an outrage.

There was no need to lead her. She went with Eteoneus. There was noise and trouble and tears enough about roping up the others and it felt long to Yellowhead before it was over. He kept his eyes off Helen. What should his eyes say to hers? Yet how could they say nothing? He busied himself picking out the men who were to be the prisoners' escort.

At last. The women and, for the moment, the problem, were gone.

'Come on, lads,' he said. 'We must be busy again. We must go right through the castle and meet the others. Don't fancy it's all over.'

He longed to be fighting again. He would fight as he'd never fought before. Perhaps he would be killed. Then the army could do what they pleased with her. For that dim and mostly comfortable picture of a future which hovers before most men's eyes had vanished.

III

The first thing Yellowhead knew next morning was the burning of the cut above his knee. Then he stretched and felt the after-battle ache in every muscle; swallowed once or twice and found he was very thirsty; sat up, and found his elbow was bruised. The door of the hut was open and he could tell by the light that it was hours after sunrise. Two thoughts hung in his mind— the war is over—Helen is here. Not much emotion about either.

He got up, grunting a little, rubbed his eyes, and went out into the open. Inland, he saw the smoke hanging in still air above the ruins of Troy, and, lower down, innumerable birds. Everything was shockingly quiet. The army must be sleeping late.

Eteoneus, limping a little and wearing a bandage on his right hand, came towards him.

'Have you any water left?' said Menelaus. 'My throat's as dry as that sand.'

'You'll have to have wine in it, Yellowhead Menelaus. We've wine enough to swim in, but we're nearly out of water.'

Menelaus made a face. 'Make it as weak as you can,' he said.

Eteoneus limped away and returned with the cup. Both went into the King's hut and Eteoneus pulled the door to.

'What did you do that for?' said Yellowhead.

'We have to talk, Menelaus.'

'Talk? I think I'll sleep again.'

'Look,' said Eteoneus, 'here's something you ought to know. When Agathocles brought all our share of the women down last night, he penned the rest of them in the big hut where we've been keeping the horses. He picketed the horses outside—safe enough now. But he put the Queen by herself in the hut beyond this.'

'*Queen*, you call her? How do you know she's going to be a queen much longer? I haven't given any orders. I haven't made up my mind.'

'No, but the men have.'

'What do you mean?'

'That's what they call her. And they call her Daughter of Zeus. And they saluted her hut when they went past it.'

'Well, of all the——'

'Listen, Menelaus. It's no use at all thinking about your anger. You *can't* treat her as anything but your Queen. The men won't stand it.'

'But, gates of Hades, I thought the whole army was longing for her blood! After all they've been through because of her.'

'The army in general, yes. But not our own Spartans. She's still the Queen to them.'

'That? That faded, fat, old trot? Paris's cast-off whore and the gods know whose besides? Are they mad? What's Helen to them? Has every one forgotten that it's I who am her husband and her king, and their king too, curse them?'

'If you want me to answer that, I must say something that's not to your liking.'

'Say what you please.'

'You said you were her husband and their king. They'd say you are their king only because you're her husband. You're not of the blood royal of Sparta. You became their king by marrying her. Your kingship hangs on her queenship.'

Yellowhead snatched up an empty scabbard and hit savagely

three or four times at a wasp that was hovering above a spilled wine-drop. 'Cursed, cursed creature!' he yelled. 'Can't I kill even you? Perhaps you're sacred too. Perhaps Eteoneus here will cut my throat if I swot you. There! There!'

He did not get the wasp. When he sat down again he was sweating.

'I knew it wouldn't please you,' said Eteoneus, 'but——'

'It was the wasp that put me out of patience,' said Yellow-head. 'Do you think I'm such a fool as not to know how I got my own throne? Do you think *that* galls me? I thought you knew me better. Of course they're right; in law. But no one ever takes notice of these things once a marriage has been made.'

Eteoneus said nothing.

'Do you mean,' said Yellowhead, 'that they've been thinking that way all the time?'

'It never came up before. How should it? But they never forgot about her being the daughter of the highest god.'

'Do you believe it?'

'Till I know what it pleases the gods to have said about it, I'll keep my tongue between my teeth.'

'And then,' said Yellowhead, jabbing once more at the wasp, 'there's this. If she was really the daughter of Zeus she wouldn't be the daughter of Tyndareus. She'd be no nearer the true line than I am.'

'I suppose they'd think Zeus a greater king than either you or Tyndareus.'

'And so would you,' said Yellowhead, grinning.

'Yes,' said Eteoneus. Then, 'I've had to speak out, Son of Atreus. It's a question of my own life as well as yours. If you set our men fighting-mad against you, you know very well I'll be with you back to back, and they won't slit your throat till they've slit mine.'

A loud, rich, happy voice, a voice like an uncle's, was heard singing outside. The door opened. There stood Agamemnon. He was in his best armour, all the bronze newly polished, and the cloak on his shoulders was scarlet, and his beard gleaming with sweet oil. The other two looked like beggars in his presence. Eteoneus rose and bowed to the King of Men. Yellowhead nodded to his brother.

'Well, Yellowhead,' said Agamemnon. 'How are you? Send your squire for some wine.' He strode into the hut and ruffled the curls on his brother's head as if they were a child's. 'What cheer? You don't look like a sacker of cities. Moping? Haven't we won a victory? And got your prize back, eh?' He gave a chuckle that shook the whole of his big chest.

'What are you laughing at?' said Yellowhead.

'Ah, the wine,' said Agamemnon, taking the cup from Eteoneus's hand. He drank at length, put the cup down, sucked his wet moustache, and said, 'No wonder you're glum, brother. I've seen our prize. Took a look into her hut. Gods!' He threw his head back and laughed his full.

'I don't know that you and I have any need to talk about my wife,' said Yellowhead.

'Indeed we have,' said Agamemnon. 'For the matter of that, it might have been better if we'd talked about her before you married. I might have given you some advice. You don't know how to handle women. When a man does know, there's never any trouble. Look at me now. Ever heard of Clytemnestra giving me any trouble? She knows better.'

'You said we had to talk now, not all those years ago.'

'I'm coming to that. The question is what's to be done about this woman. And, by the way, what do you *want* to do?'

'I haven't made up my mind. I suppose it's my own business.'

'Not entirely. The army has made up its mind, you see.'

'What's it to do with them?'

'Will you never grow up? Haven't they been told all these years that she's the cause of the whole thing—of their friends' deaths and their own wounds and the gods only know what troubles waiting for them when they get home? Didn't we keep on telling them we were fighting to get Helen back? Don't they want to make her pay for it?'

'It would be far truer to say they were fighting for me. Fighting to get me my wife. The gods know that's true. Don't rub that wound. I wouldn't blame the army if they killed me. I didn't want it this way. I'd rather have gone with a handful of my own men and taken my chance. Even when we got here I tried to settle it by a single combat. You know I did. But if it comes to——'

'There, there, there, Yellowhead. Don't start blaming yourself all over again. We've heard it before. And if it's any comfort to you, I see no harm in telling you (now the thing's over) that you weren't quite as important in starting the war as you seem to think. Can't you understand that Troy had to be crushed? We couldn't go on having her sitting there at the gate to the Euxine, levying tolls on Greek ships and sinking Greek ships and putting up the price of corn. The war had to come.'

'Do you mean I—and Helen—were just pretexts? If I'd thought——'

'Brother, you make everything so childishly simple. Of course I wanted to avenge your honour, and the honour of Greece. I was bound to by my oaths. And I also knew—all the Greek kings who had any sense knew—that we had to make an end of Troy. But it was a windfall—a gift from the gods—that Paris ran off with your wife at exactly the right moment.'

'Then I'd thank you to have told the army the truth at the very outset.'

'My boy, we told them the part of the truth that they would care about. Avenging a rape and recovering the most beautiful woman in the world—that's the sort of thing the troops can understand and will fight for. What would be the use of talking to them about the corn-trade? You'll never make a general.'

'I'll have some wine too, Eteoneus,' said Yellowhead. He drank it fiercely when it was brought and said nothing.

'And now,' continued Agamemnon, 'now they've got her, they'll want to see her killed. Probably want to cut her throat on Achilles' tomb.'

'Agamemnon,' said Eteoneus, 'I don't know what Menelaus

means to do. But the rest of us Spartans will fight if there's any attempt to kill the Queen.'

'And you think I'd sit by and watch?' said Menelaus, looking angrily at him. 'If it comes to fighting, I'll be your leader still.'

'This is very pretty,' said Agamemnon. 'But you are both so hasty. I came, Yellowhead, to tell you that the army will almost certainly demand Helen for the priest's knife. I half expected you'd say "Good riddance" and hand her over. But then I'd have had to tell you something else. When they see her, as she now is, I don't think they'll believe it is Helen at all. That's the real danger. They'll think you have a beautiful Helen—the Helen of their dreams—safely hidden away. There'll be a meeting. And you'll be the man they'll go for.'

'Do they expect a girl to look the same after ten years?' said Yellowhead.

'Well, I was a bit surprised when I saw her myself,' said Agamemnon. 'And I've a notion that you were too.' (He repeated his detestable chuckle.) 'Of course we may pass some other prisoner off as Helen. There are some remarkably pretty girls. Or even if they weren't quite convinced, it might keep them quiet; provided they thought the real Helen was unobtainable. So it all comes to this. If you want you and your Spartans and the woman to be safe, there's only one way. You must all embark quietly tonight and leave me to play my hand alone. I'll do better without you.'

'You'll have done better without me all your life.'

'Not a bit, not a bit. I go home as the Sacker of Troy. Think of Orestes growing up with that to back him! Think of the husbands I'll be able to get for my girls! Poor Clytemnestra will like it too. I shall be a happy man.'

IV

I only want justice. And to be let alone. From the very beginning, from the day I married Helen down to this moment, who can say I've done him a wrong? I had a right to marry her.

Tyndareus gave her to me. He even asked the girl herself and she made no objection. What fault could she find in me after I was her husband? I never struck her. I never rated her. I very seldom even had one of the housegirls to my bed, and no sensible woman makes a fuss about that. Did I ever take her child from her and sacrifice it to the Storm-gods? Yet Agamemnon does that, and has a faithful, obedient wife.

Did I ever work my way into another man's house and steal his woman? Paris does that to me. I try to have my revenge in the right way, single combat before both armies. Then there's some divine interference—a kind of black-out—I don't know what happened to me—and he has escaped. I was winning. He was as good as dead man if I'd had two minutes more. Why do the gods never interfere on the side of the man who was wronged?

I never fought against gods as Diomede did, or says he did. I never turned against our own side and worked for the defeat of the Greeks, like Achilles. And now he's a god and they make his tomb an altar. I never shirked like Odysseus, I never committed sacrilege like Odysseus. And now he's the real captain of them all—Agamemnon for all his winks and knowingness couldn't rule the army for a day without him—and I'm nothing.

Nothing and nobody. I thought I was the King of Sparta. Apparently I'm the only one who ever thought so. I am simply that woman's head servant. I'm to fight her wars and collect her tribute and do all her work, but she's the Queen. She can turn whore, turn traitress, turn Trojan. That makes no difference. The moment she's in our camp she is Queen just as before. All the archers and horseboys can tell me to mend my manners and take care I treat her majesty with proper respect. Even Eteoneus—my own sworn brother—taunts me with being no true king. Then next moment he says he'll die with me if the Spartans decide I'd better be murdered. I wonder. Probably he's a traitor too. Perhaps he's this raddled Queen's next lover.

Not a king. It's worse than that. I'm not even a freeman. Any hired man, any peddlar, any beggar, would be allowed to teach his own wife a lesson, if she'd been false to him, in the way he thought best. For me it's Hands Off. She's the Queen, the Daughter of Zeus.

And then comes Agamemnon sneering—just as he always did ever since we were boys—and making jokes because she's lost her beauty. What right has he to talk to me about her like that? I wonder what his own Clytemnestra looks like now. Ten years, ten years. And they must have had short commons in Troy for some time. Unhealthy too, cooped up inside the walls. Lucky there seems to have been no plague. And who knows how those barbarians treated her once the war began to turn against them? By Hera, I must find out about that. When I can talk to her. Can I talk to her? How would I begin?

Eteoneus worships her, and Agamemnon jeers at her, and the army wants to cut her throat. Whose woman is she? Whose business is she? Everyone's except mine, it seems. I count for nothing. I'm a bit of her property and she's a bit of everyone else's.

I've been a puppet in a war about corn-ships.

I wonder what she's thinking herself. Alone all those hours in that hut. Wondering and wondering, no doubt. Unless she's giving an audience to Eteoneus.

Shall we get away safely tonight? We've done all we can do by daylight. Nothing to do but wait.

Perhaps it would be best if the army got wind of it and we were all killed, fighting, on the beach. She and Eteoneus would see there's one thing I can still do. I'd kill her before they took her. Punish her and save her with one stroke.

Curse these flies.

V

(Later. Landed in Egypt and entertained by an Egyptian.)

'I'm sorry you've asked for that, Father,' said Menelaus. 'But you said it to spare me. Indeed, indeed, the woman's not worth your having.'

'The cold water a man wants is better than the wine he's no taste for,' said the old man.

'I'd give something better than such cold water. I beseech you to accept this cup. The Trojan King drank from it himself.'

'Will you deny me the woman, Guest?' said the old man, still smiling.

'You must pardon me, Father,' said Menelaus. 'I'd be ashamed——'

'She's the thing I ask for.'

'Curse these barbarians and their ways,' thought Menelaus to himself. 'Is this a courtesy of theirs? Is it the rule always to ask for something of no value?'

'You will not deny me surely?' said his host, still not looking at Helen, but looking sidelong at Menelaus.

'He really wants her,' Menelaus thought. It began to make him angry.

'If you won't give her,' said the Egyptian, a little scornfully, 'perhaps you'll sell.'

Menelaus felt his face reddening. He had found a reason for his anger now: it accordingly grew hotter. The man was insulting him.

'I tell you the woman's not for giving,' he said. 'And a thousand times not for selling.'

The old man showed no anger—could that smooth, brown face ever show it?—and kept on smiling.

'Ah,' he said at last, drawing it out very long. 'You should have told me. She is perhaps your old nurse or——'

'She's my wife,' Menelaus shouted. The words came out of his mouth, loud, boyish, and ridiculous; he hadn't meant to say them at all. He darted his eyes round the room. If anyone laughed he'd kill them. But all the Egyptian faces were grave, though anyone could see that the minds within them were mocking him. His own men sat with their eyes on the floor. They were ashamed of him.

'Stranger,' said the old man. 'Are you sure that woman is your wife?'

Menelaus glanced sharply towards Helen, half believing for the moment that these foreign wizards might have played some trick. The glance was so quick that it caught hers and for the first time their eyes met. And indeed she was changed. He surprised a look of what seemed to be, of all things, joy. In the name of the House of Hades, why? It passed in an instant; the set desolation returned. But now his host was speaking again.

'I know very well who your wife is, Menelaus son of Atreus. You married Helen Tyndaris. And that woman is not she.'

'But this is madness,' said Menelaus. 'Do you think I don't know?'

'That is indeed what I think,' replied the old man, now wholly grave. 'Your wife never went to Troy. The gods have played a trick with you. That woman was in Troy. That woman lay in Paris's bed. Helen was caught away.'

'Who is that, then?' said Menelaus.

'Ah, who could answer? It is a thing—it will soon go away—such things sometimes go about the earth for a while. No one knows what they are.'

'You are making fun of me,' said Menelaus. He did not think so; still less did he believe what he was told. He thought he was out of his right mind; drunk perhaps, or else the wine had been drugged.

'It is no wonder if you say that,' replied the host. 'But you will not say it when I have shown you the real Helen.'

Menelaus sat still. He had the sense that some outrage was being done to him. One could not argue with these foreign devils. He had never been clever. If Odysseus had been here he would have known what to say. Meanwhile the musicians resumed their playing. The slaves, cat-footed, were moving about. They were moving the lights all into one place, over on the far side near a doorway, so that the rest of the large hall grew darker and darker and one looked painfully at the glare of the clustered candles. The music went on.

'Daughter of Leda, come forth,' said the old man.

And at once it came. Out of the darkness of the doorway

NOTES TO *AFTER TEN YEARS*

I

ROGER LANCELYN GREEN

This story of Helen and Menelaus after the fall of Troy was started, and the first chapter written in, I think, 1959—before Lewis's visit to Greece. It began, as Lewis wrote that the Narnian stories began and grew, from 'seeing pictures' in his mind—the picture of Yellow-head *in* the Wooden Horse and the realization of what he and the rest must have experienced during almost twenty-four hours of claustrophobia, discomfort, and danger. I remember him reading to me the first chapter, and the thrill of the growing knowledge of where we were and who Yellowhead was.

But Lewis had not worked out any plot for the rest of the story. We discussed all the legends of Helen and Menelaus that either of us knew—and I was rather 'up' in Trojan matters at the time, as I was writing my own story *The Luck of Troy* which ends where Lewis's begins. I remember pointing out that Menelaus was only King of Sparta on account of his marriage with Helen, who was the heiress of Tyndareus (after the death of Castor and Polydeuces)—a point which Lewis did not know, but seized upon eagerly and used in the next chapters.

He read the rest of the fragment to me in August 1960, after our visit to Greece—and after Joy's (his wife) death. The Egyptian scrap came later still, I think: but after that year Lewis found that he could no longer make up stories—nor go on with this one. It was because of this drying up of the imaginative spring (perhaps the inability to 'see pictures' any longer) that he planned to collaborate with me in a new version of my story *The Wood that Time Forgot* which I had written about 1950 and which Lewis always said was my best— though no publisher would risk it. But this was late 1962 and early 1963—and nothing came of it.

Naturally it is not possible to be certain what Lewis would have done in *After Ten Years* if he had gone on with it: he did not know himself—and we discussed so many possibilities that I cannot even be certain which he preferred.

The next 'picture' after the scene in the Horse was the idea of what Helen must really have looked like after ten years as a captive in besieged Troy. Of course the Classical authors—Quintus Smyrnaeus, Tryphiodorus, Apollodorus, etc.—insist on her divine beauty remaining unimpaired. Some authors say that Menelaus drew his sword to kill her after Troy had fallen, then saw her beauty, and the sword fell from his hand; others say that the soldiers were preparing to stone her—but she let fall her veil, and they dropped the stones and worshipped instead of slaying. Her beauty excused all: 'To Heracles Zeus gave strength, to Helen beauty, which naturally rules over even strength itself,' wrote Isocrates—and as I pointed out to Lewis, Helen returned to Sparta with Menelaus and was not only the beautiful Queen who welcomes Telemachus in the *Odyssey*, but was worshipped as a goddess, whose shrine may still be seen at Theraphai near Sparta.

However the scrap of the story set in Egypt is based on the legend begun by Stesichorus and developed by Euripides in his play *Helena* that Helen never went to Troy at all. On the way, she and Paris stopped in Egypt, and the gods fashioned an imitation Helen, an 'Eidolon', a thing of air, which Paris took to Troy, thinking it was the real Helen. For this phantom the Greeks fought and Troy fell. On his return (and he took nearly as long to get home as Odysseus) Menelaus visited Egypt: and there the Eidolon vanished and he found the true Helen, lovely and unsullied, and took *her* back to Sparta with him. (This legend gave Rider Haggard and Andrew Lang the idea for their romance of Helen in Egypt, *The World's Desire*—though it was set some years after the end of the *Odyssey*— a book which Lewis read and admired, even if he did not value it quite as highly as I do.)

The idea which Lewis was following—or with which he was experimenting—was a 'twist' of the Eidolon legend. 'Out of the darkness of the doorway' came the beautiful Helen whom Menelaus had originally married—Helen so beautiful that she must have been the daughter of Zeus—the dream beauty whose image Menelaus had built up during the ten years of the siege of Troy, and which had been so cruelly shattered when he found Helen in Chapter II. *But* this was the Eidolon: the story was to turn on the conflict between dream and reality. It was to be a development of the *Mary Rose* theme, again with a twist: Mary Rose comes back after many years in Fairyland, but exactly as on the moment of her disappearance— her husband and parents have thought of her, longed for her, like this—but when she does return, she just doesn't fit.

Menelaus had dreamed of Helen, longed for Helen, built up his image of Helen and worshipped it as a false idol: in Egypt he is offered that idol, the Eidolon. I don't think he was to know which was the true Helen, but of this I am not certain. But I think he was to discover in the end that the middle-aged, faded Helen he had brought from Troy was the real woman, and between them was the real love or its possibility: the Eidolon would have been a *Belle Dame sans merci* . . .

But I repeat that I do not know—and Lewis did not know—what exactly would have happened if he had gone on with the story.

II

ALASTAIR FOWLER

Lewis spoke more than once about the difficulties he was having with this story. He had a clear idea of the kind of narrative he wanted to write, of the theme, and of the characters; but he was unable to get beyond the first few chapters. As his habit was in such cases, he put the piece aside and went on with something else. From the fragment written, one might expect that the continuation would have been a myth of very general import. For the dark belly of the horse could be taken as a womb, the escape from it as a birth and entry on life. Lewis was well aware of this aspect. But he said that the idea for the book was provoked by Homer's tantalizingly brief account of the relationship between Menelaus and Helen after the return from Troy (*Od.* iv 1–305). It was, I suppose, a moral as much as a literary idea. Lewis wanted to tell the story of a cuckold in such a way as to bring out the meaningfulness of his life. In the eyes of others Menelaus might seem to have lost almost all that was honourable and heroic; but in his own he had all that mattered: love. Naturally, the treatment of such a theme entailed a narrative stand-point very different from Homer's. And this is already apparent in the present fragment: instead of looking on the horse from without as we do when Demodocus sings (*Od.* viii 499–520), here we feel something of the difficult life inside.